seinfeld

THE TOTALLY UNAUTHORIZED TRIBUTE
[not that there's anything wrong with that]

seinfeld

THE TOTALLY UNAUTHORIZED TRIBUTE
[not that there's anything wrong with that]

BY DAVID WILD

THREE RIVERS PRESS
NEW YORK

Published by Three Rivers Press, a division of Crown Publishers, Inc., 201 East 50th Street, New York, New York 10022. Member of the Crown Publishing Group.

Random House, Inc. New York, Toronto, London, Sydney, Auckland
www.randomhouse.com

THREE RIVERS PRESS and colophon are trademarks of Crown Publishers, Inc.

Printed in the United States of America

Design by Blond on Pond/Kay Schuckhart

Library of Congress Cataloging-in-Publication Data
Wild, David, 1961–
    Seinfeld : the totally unauthorized tribute (not that there's
anything wrong with that) / by David Wild. — 1st pbk. ed.
    1. Seinfeld—Miscellanea.   I. Title
PN1992.77.S4285W56   1998
791.45'72—dc21   97–44145

ISBN 0-609-80311-5

10 9 8 7 6 5 4 3 2

First Edition

contents

acknowledgments

Much like the Holy Bible, Geoffrey Chaucer's *Canterbury Tales,* Dante Alighieri's *The Divine Comedy,* Marcel Proust's *Remembrance of Things Past,* Franz Kafka's *The Metamorphosis,* James Joyce's *Ulysses,* F. Scott Fitzgerald's *The Great Gatsby,* Gabriel García Márquez's *One Hundred Years of Solitude* or even Jerry Seinfeld's sacred text *SeinLanguage,* this small three-dimensional rectangular object you now hold in your hands is a book—a professionally bound affair featuring assorted words of varying lengths printed on pieces of paper.

There are, however, some less immediately apparent but nonetheless crucial differences between this semihumble effort and all those earlier, time-tested masterpieces. Unlike those works of art, this is not the sort of book that springs full-born from the overactive muse of a creative genius. Instead, in the spirit of limited friendship that is at the ambivalent but functioning heart of *Seinfeld,* I needed more than a smidgen of help from my friends along the way. Therefore I must take this opportunity to thank a number of people who helped make *Seinfeld: The Totally Unauthorized Tribute (Not That There's Anything Wrong with That)* such a gala affair, even though it must be noted that actually acknowledging the contributions of others cannot be said to be a top concern of *Seinfeld*'s hilariously self-obsessed characters.

Lisa San Miguel and Dana Meltzer provided invaluable editorial research. Thanks also go to all those journalists who have gone before me in writing about *Seinfeld,* to the Academy of Motion Picture Arts and Sciences Library and to the helpful staff of the Museum of Television and Radio in Beverly Hills for their excellent video library and their effective air-conditioning. Furthermore, though her fee gets paid first, I nonetheless remain forever indebted to Sarah Lazin of Sarah Lazin Books for her ace agentry and caring support. For this project, I also had the pleasure of getting to know and collaborating with Kristin Kiser, my gifted and forthright editor— a woman of letters who's sort of like Elaine Benes at Pendant Publishing, only with less neurosis and even more amazing Jackie O–like grace. Thanks as always to all of my family and everyone at *Rolling Stone* and the Wenner Media mothership. Obviously, without the enduringly great and inspiring work of everyone involved in the creation of *Seinfeld* there would be little point in creating this sort of tribute. It is with great pride and a modicum of dignity that I bow down before them, since they truly are the masters of their televised domain.

Finally, however, this is for the ultimate master of my domain, my beloved son, Andrew Dylan Wild, who was born to my wife, Fran, and me during the birth process of this book. The lucky little guy—who has significantly more hair than myself and George Costanza combined—was fortunate enough to watch a *Seinfeld* rerun during his very first day on earth. From the timing of his adorable, guttural cooing, I believe he may have already identified himself as firstly an Elaine man—of course, his selection process may very well have something to do with the fact that she remains the character who appeared the

most ripe for breast-feeding, more so even than Newman.

Whatever *Seinfeld* character Andrew eventually chooses as his favorite when he grows up, my wife and I pledge to support his decision with a love even more unconditional than Helen Seinfeld's for her own baby boy. As Jerry's mom has often asked regarding her son, how could anyone *not* love him? Finally, being with Andrew is the only better way to spend a half hour than watching *Seinfeld*, though in all fairness to the show, unlike our dearest son, watching *Seinfeld* has *never* to my knowledge yet been involved in any documented incidents of projectile peeing—*not that there's anything wrong with that!*

THE TOTALLY UNAUTHORIZED TRIBUTE

[not that there's anything wrong with that]

Stand-Up Guy: Jerry Seinfeld in his natural environment.

PRE-YADA

SEINFELD, OUR SHOW OF SHOWS

Like other viewers of a certain vintage, I watched a lot of TV in the relatively dreary pre-*Seinfeld* era, but television at that time just didn't mean that much to me. Hey, I *liked* Lucy, but I cannot in good faith say I ever truly *loved* that groundbreaking witchy woman Elizabeth Montgomery than any pure comedy aesthetics.

I've been a friend of *Friends,* a respectful colleague of *Frasier,* an occasional teetotaling patron at *Cheers,* a fussy if patient follower of *ER* and a *Nightline* groupie, as well as a resident

> ## "They think they're doing Samuel Beckett instead of a sitcom."
>
> *—Fighting words from Roseanne Arnold—as she was known at the time—attacking the* Seinfeld *cast for taking on pretentious airs in the midst of the great* Seinfeld-Roseanne *parking space war of 1993*

redhead. By the same token, I never quite felt part of *All in the Family* either despite my genuine admiration for both the Bunker and Stivic sitcom clans. Rare too was the night I dreamt of Jeannie, although I openly confess to often feeling *Bewitched*—but in truth that fuzzy and warm sensation was ultimately much more about preadolescent lust for alien who has always been more than happy to waste hours explaining the phenomenon of *The X-Files.*

Though I am now in the thick of my thirtysomething years and actually old enough to have fathered at least one of the members of Hanson, I am still way too young to have enjoyed the original *Your Show of Shows*—the legendary Sid

Caesar–hosted NBC comedy series of the fifties that many consider a high-water mark of the early days of TV. And so it is that for millions of us who are like-minded at least in this single respect, a show called *Seinfeld* has climbed to the top of our pop culture pantheon and become *our* show of shows.

For the faithful around the world, *Seinfeld*—the world of Jerry, George, Elaine, Kramer and the other assorted misfits in their lives of not-so-quiet desperation—is at the comic center of the universe. And despite some predictions to the contrary, the funny truths that the show tells have proven remarkably universal, though many dedicated followers of all things *Seinfeld*-ian have never pounded the semi-mean streets of the Upper West Side, the neighborhood where the show largely takes place, nor would they claim any affinity for the Big Apple.

I lived on the Upper West Side back when *Seinfeld* first hit the airwaves, but these days I reside in Los Angeles only a few miles up the hill from the *Seinfeld* soundstage at the CBS Radford Studios in Studio City. Here in Tinseltown, syndicated showings of *Seinfeld* run weekday evenings at 7:30 on the same channel that broadcasts many far less entertaining and winning Dodgers baseball games. And while I love Abner Doubleday's invention as much as the proverbial next guy, often around 7:15

P.M. during baseball season I find myself praying for a sudden rain-out or some other act of God to intervene so that the game won't stop me from enjoying America's real favorite pastime—watching and reveling in syndicated *Seinfeld*.

For those of us fortunate enough to pass our time with *Seinfeld*, it has become the series against which everything else seeking to be sitcomical must be judged and inevitably found wanting. *Seinfeld* is popular art of the highest order. Television ratings reflect the fact that there's a huge audience out there that will turn up to watch *Seinfeld* as often as they're offered the opportunity. Yet remarkably, while the show has become part of our cultural vocabulary and a fixture in millions of lives, it still manages to retain the unique qualities that made the series stand out in the first place—its comic bite, its self-flagellating bile and its consistent brilliance.

Back in those glorious if vacuous mid- to late eighties, a relatively carefree age when O.J. was a beverage and grunge simply dirt, I found myself a regular audience member at the Comic Strip, a popular comedy club on Manhattan's East Side. I was then—as now—employed at *Rolling Stone* magazine, and with all the rock concerts I had to attend for my work, going to comedy clubs provided a great break and much-needed

SEINING OFF
MICHAEL J. FOX on *Seinfeld*

*On the day he was nominated for an Emmy in 1997 to honor his fine work in the
ABC series* Spin City, *Michael J. Fox took time out to pay tribute to one of his own favorite shows,*
Seinfeld. *Later, at the Emmys, Jerry Seinfeld would comment memorably on Fox taking away
his slot in the Lead Actor in a Comedy Series nomination. "I guess last year you people didn't buy me as
me," Seinfeld joked. Fox definitely buys* Seinfeld *big time, as he makes eminently clear.*

Seinfeld radically altered the framework of situation comedy. For me it was interesting, because I
was on TV for seven years with *Family Ties*, then I went away. And when I came back it was a whole
different and much more exciting ball game for him having been here. The idea of busting out all
the walls really came from *Seinfeld*. In *Family Ties*, we used to do three scenes, then an act break,
then three scenes and then Alex apologizes. And when I came back with *Spin City*, we now do like
twenty scenes. The ability to sort of free-associate with scenes—completely out of the standard
decrepit structure—is Jerry Seinfeld and Larry David's doing. There was almost a feeling—and it
was thrilling for me as a member of the audience—that I was kind of irrelevant. What my expecta-
tion was, or whether I was being patronized, or condescended to or being spoken up to, I didn't get
the sense they gave a shit. That was a thrill. It was like, we're going to do this *regardless*.

I think *Seinfeld* raised the bar on what writers could do. If you've ever seen a table of sitcom writers, there was always a time when it deteriorated into silliness, a period when it's like eleven o'clock
and the Chinese food has hit like a bomb and they start getting goofy and doing a lot of stuff that
doesn't go anywhere. Then the executive producer usually comes in. But you sense with *Seinfeld*,
that's when the writers *start* working. That was the stuff they brought to the audience. Writers were
told *not* to do that stuff—we don't talk about soup nazis and masturbation, but they said, "That's
funny." My favorite episode is the one with George banging the cleaning lady on his desk. *[Author's
note: "The Red Dot."]* The classic scene is the one with George and the boss afterwards, and the boss
being outraged, with George saying something to the effect of, "Oh, that's *not* allowed then. So now
I know." Then he gives her the marked-down sweater. I thought that episode was just great.

So do you consider yourself a George man?

I love the show as a whole in the same way that you love the Beatles as a whole. Would George be
John? Because I was always a Lennon guy, I think George would be John because on some level he
didn't give a shit. Kramer is Ringo. Dreyfus would be George. And that would mean Jerry is Paul,
right?

A *SEINFELD* CASE HISTORY ABOUT NOTHING

Want to know how entertaining *Seinfeld* is? Not only is the show itself an outright TV classic, even litigation in which our show figures prominently turns out to be required viewing too. In the summer of 1997, just in time to keep the world occupied during those dreaded summer repeats, the case of *Mackenzie* v. *Miller Brewing Co.* saved us from boredom as it was broadcast in all its glory on Court TV. If *Seinfeld* really was a show about nothing, this strange brew of litigation sometimes appeared to be a case about nothing.

It seems that on March 18, 1993, a manager at Miller Brewing, one Jerold J. Mackenzie—who I would guess is a George man—had caught most of *Seinfeld* episode 58, "The Junior Mint," in which Jerry cannot remember the name of his love interest, other than that her first name rhymes with a part of the female anatomy. Her name, as we would all discover at the end of the episode, was not Mulva, as Jerry guessed at one point, but rather Delores.

The next morning, Mackenzie was at his job in Wisconsin, and he asked a coworker named Patricia Best if she had seen the episode. She had not, and Mackenzie ended up expressing his astonishment that the show had made it past the censors. He asked Best to guess what word rhymed with Delores. She could not. And after further discussion about the episode with another coworker, Mackenzie—apparently not wanting to use the word *clitoris* aloud—instead copied the page from the dictionary with the term and proceeded to show it to Best. Now, it could be argued that any show that has Americans rushing to the dictionary ought to be saluted as educational programming, but it appears that Best did not feel similarly.

On March 23, after a long weekend, Best reported the conversation to David Goulet, Mackenzie's immediate superior. Goulet suggested a number of options, one of which was for Best to confront Mackenzie herself. She did so, and Mackenzie apologized while also expressing his disbelief that he would have offended someone who was known to use vulgar language herself. This encounter was reported by Best back to Goulet, who then brought the issue to the company's personnel department.

Now, in some companies, this sort of tempest in a beer keg might have gone straight into the Pensky File and disappeared forever, but not at the Miller Brewing Co. The next day Mackenzie was invited to the company's law library, where he was questioned regarding the incident by a lawyer representing the company. That same day he was fired by the brewery for "unacceptable managerial performance" and escorted out of the building.

Mackenzie responded by suing Miller Brewing Co., Patricia Best and his former supervisor Robert Smith, a Miller vice president. According to Court TV's case file on America Online, Mackenzie alleged that "his firing was improper, the coworker was not harassed and the company was looking for an excuse to terminate him."

Jurors—who consisted of Americans and thus must have included at least a few *Seinfeld* fans in their number—ultimately decided on July 15, 1997, to award Mackenzie $26.6 million. In the July 28, 1997, edition of *Time* magazine, a twenty-year-old juror named Clint Baer revealed that none of the twelve jurors, ten of whom were women, were offended by the mildly racy *Seinfeld* plotline. For the record, it appears that Kramer's favorite Johnnie Cochran–esque attorney, Jackie Chiles, who first surfaced in "The Maestro," played absolutely no role in these proceedings. The whole matter was almost enough to make you believe in the jury system.

change of pace. At least these people riffing solo onstage with just a microphone for accompaniment at the Comic Strip were *trying* to be funny.

Cultural historians will someday tell us that this period was the Golden Age of Stand-Up Comedy, a jokey boom period when magazine article after magazine article predicted that comedy was on the verge of becoming the rock and roll of the nineties. At the time it seemed unclear if rock and roll would then become the comedy of the nineties, though the recent massive success of the Spice Girls suggests that this is indeed the case.

My own favorite comedian whom I would see at the Comic Strip then was an unpretentious but hilarious fellow by the name of Jerry Seinfeld. He was quick. He was confident. He was sharp. He was, relative to the norm in the scumbaggy world of comedy clubs, almost wholesome but never bland. He was what Grammy Hall would call a real Jew. He was polished, with extraordinary timing, a man full of odd but true insights, a low-key observational genius.

I can remember thinking Jerry Seinfeld was consistently the funniest man I had ever seen. I can also remember guessing that he would most likely never be a big deal beyond the boroughs. At the time, Robin Williams was our frantic king of comedy, while Andrew Dice Clay and Sam Kinison were venom-spewing up-and-comers. What chance did this bittersweet *hamisha* homeboy from Long Island have of scoring the spotlight in humor's big leagues?

In retrospect, of course, I need not have worried too terribly much about this Seinfeld character's prospects. As evidenced by the fact that he now reaps a considerable part of the gross national product, it turns out that Jerry Seinfeld could handle himself just fine in the big bad world of comedy. If he was "too New York" or "too Jewish" for prime time, he somehow managed to find a bridge to the mainstream by way of pure quality. He has been able to find the Big Apple within all hearts, and he's become, if not everyman, at least a universally appealing everyjew.

Unlike the *Friends* cast, who were unfairly singled out for being well paid in show biz, there was little public disgust about Jerry Seinfeld's far more gargantuan deal. Like his longtime pal Jay Leno, Seinfeld is famous for his comic work ethic—he would sometimes do more than three hundred stand-up gigs a year in the old days, and since the departure of his partner Larry David, he's taken on ultimate responsibility of maintaining the quality of *Seinfeld*. When *Forbes* magazine came out with their annual list of the forty best-paid entertainers in 1997, Jerry Seinfeld landed in the sixth position with estimated 1996–1997 earnings of $94 million, sandwiching him between the fifth-place Beatles at $98 million and—there goes the fiscal neighborhood—magic man David Copperfield, who by some sleight of hand earned seventh place by making $85 million appear. Still, insomuch as anyone in his field can be said to deserve what they make, Seinfeld has made his many millions the old-fashioned way—he's *earned* it.

A few years back I had the great fiscal and emotional pleasure of penning an important tome entitled *Friends: The Official Companion*. This seminal text—

other facets of our *Friends* society. Through all my promotional travels—the good, the bad, the ugly and the dopey—people would suggest other TV books I should write next. One young man in a jester's cap who attended my book signing at a Barnes and Noble superstore in Rancho Cucamonga, California, felt strongly that I should get right to work on a *Saved by the Bell* book.

Now I, like all good Americans, have nothing but the greatest respect for the legacy of Screech and company, but these words gave me a bad case of semiliterary

Seinfeld is one of those rare redeemers of popular culture; like Sinatra, pasta or the Beatles, *Seinfeld* shows that sometimes the masses get things exactly right.

which became a surprise best-seller (at least it was a surprise to me)—has been described by one writer as being "much like *War and Peace*, only with many more pictures of Courteney Cox." I know this because I was the one writer who described it that way during the book's extended season of hype. Believe it or not, I was soon invited and, more significantly, paid to travel the U.S. speaking at otherwise respectable institutions of higher learning about the deeper primal meanings of Marcel the Monkey and

chills. What I told that young man—and what I told many college students who made different suggestions—was that there was only one other current show that I could imagine taking the time and effort to focus on at book length.

That show is, of course, *Seinfeld.*

Though technically the *Seinfeld Chronicles* pilot episode aired in the summer of 1989, *Seinfeld* is arguably *the* show of the nineties. And for me, *Seinfeld* is one of those rare redeemers of popular culture; like Sinatra, pasta or the Beatles,

Seinfeld shows that sometimes the masses get things exactly right. Could the thirty million or so American *Seinfeld* viewers who tune in each week be wrong? Well, actually, they *could* be wrong—after all, a lot of people watch *Walker, Texas Ranger,* too—but in this case the populace shows remarkably good taste and sophistication.

Way back in 1961, when I was born, Newton Norman Minow, who was then chairman of the Federal Communications Commission—the man perhaps best known for calling television "a vast wasteland"—rightly pointed out that "when television is bad, nothing is worse." Fortunately, the opposite is also true, if much too seldom applicable—when TV is really good, as it almost inevitably is on *Seinfeld,* there are few things better. Yes, on occasion, *Seinfeld* has let us down a bit by failing to live up to its own exceedingly high standards. That said, for this *Seinfeld* fan *Seinfeld* at its worst is still better and more interesting, engaging, subtle and just freakin' funnier than most other Nielsen-busting fare like, say, *Home Improvement* at the apex of its creative achievement.

While the intention behind *Seinfeld: The Totally Unauthorized Tribute (Not That There's Anything Wrong with That)* is not mere hagiography—i.e., one big written-out ass-kiss to be planted firmly on your bookshelf—I must be clear up front that this is *not* a book about nothing. Rather, this is a book about a show I

consider to be very much something, and something quite rare at that. These days I spend a considerable part of my life making fun of bad television shows in my column in *Rolling Stone,* and, trust me, media mockery can be a full-time job. Writing about *Seinfeld* gives me a chance to work the other, sunnier side of the aesthetic street.

Television—or as I prefer to call it, "That Paradox Box"—is too many things to too many people. It is said there are more than two billion TV sets out there. For some, TV is a funhouse mirror that reflects us both for better and for worse. For others, TV is a plugged-in pacifier that feeds and calms us—the tube has been called "the electronic teat," no doubt by some fancy formula-fed academic type. And in an era when the vast majority of shows leave us sadly undernourished, *Seinfeld* provides us the distinct pleasure of sucking on something of substance. The recent debate about the wisdom of a content-based ratings system for television ignored the obvious fact that as a rule there's not enough content on television to bother judging. *Seinfeld*—despite its admirable and refreshing desire to never take itself seriously—is one big exception to this rule.

The unusual public interest in and affection toward *Seinfeld* is *not* a matter of much ado about nothing. Arguably, *Seinfeld* is one hell of a lot more about *something* than most of what we watch. It's about the way we really are with our friends and the strange but true manner in which such profoundly messed-up relationships become a sort of second, more entertaining faux-dysfunctional family unit. It's about the way people now often extend adolescence well into the march to middle age. It's about great minds going to waste to brilliant comic effect. Anthropologically speaking, it's about the mores and folkways practiced by a small but fascinating tribe that's native to certain stretches of Manhattan's Upper West Side. It's about expanding the range of what TV can be about—and what TV cannot be about. For all the above reasons and a few million more, watching *Seinfeld* is still the best way to waste a little precious time in front of the television set.

My own guess is that when they sat down and started to create *Seinfeld,* Jerry Seinfeld and his then-partner Larry David were not trying to change the face of television forever. That would come in time. Rather, I think these two very different comic visionaries were more likely focused on creating something that would achieve a far higher aim—amusing *themselves.* Unlike the usual hacks whose well-appointed homes dot the Hollywood Hills, these two did not set out with the sole professional desire to pander for fun and profit. Nor did they bravely give in to the all-too-common

self-censoring instinct to ask the following logical but potentially damaging question: Is this stuff we're writing way too hip for the room called America?

Admirably, the creators of *Seinfeld* set their sights on more than a cushy syndication deal, and because Seinfeld and David were not primarily concerned with cashing in, they were able to create a show that was sufficiently original to become the first series in the history of television to earn a million dollars a minute in advertising.

So how good is *Seinfeld* exactly? Well, basically it's as good as it gets, folks. Today, nine seasons into its inspired madness as we collectively face the final curtain, the show is widely recognized as one of the best series, if not *the* best series, in all of television history. When *TV Guide* teamed up with Nick at Nite's TV Land for a *100 Greatest Episodes of All Time* special collector's issue in 1997, *Seinfeld* appeared twice on the list. The show's thirty-eighth episode, "The Parking Space"—which one hesitates to mention isn't even a particularly strong *Seinfeld*—ranked thirty-third, while the series's thirty-fourth episode, "The Boyfriend"—still probably the funniest one-hour *Seinfeld*—was ranked fourth, placing it above any of *The Honeymooners, The Dick Van Dyke Show, Cheers, The Bob Newhart Show, The X-Files* and *The Twilight Zone.* Hell, *Seinfeld* even beat *The Many Loves of Dobie Gillis.* The show has won Emmys, the prized Peabody in 1992, the American Comedy Award, Golden Globes, the Television Critics Award—basically everything except the Cy Young.

With the end of the show upon us like a hellhound, I want to pay tribute to *Seinfeld* even if that means getting paid significantly less per episode than the cast members, or even probably the show's catering staff, for that matter. I make this profound sort of personal sacrifice as a public service, because within the conventions of its sitcom form, *Seinfeld* achieves a sort of perfection. Personally, I find the most lasting episodes —like "The Contest"—as funny as anything that has preceded it coming down the cultural pipeline, be it Woody Allen, Neil Simon, Preston Sturges, Shakespeare, Jonathan Swift or even that wacky Aristophanes fellow who wrote that nutty *Frogs* sitcom.

As Jerry Seinfeld told Steve Pond in a February 1994 *TV Guide* cover story, "Funny has been hard since Aristophanes," but *Seinfeld* nearly always makes it look easy. For this lover of comic monkey business, *Seinfeld* offers a nineties equivalent to the edge and energy of the Marx Brothers. For my money *Seinfeld* is even more of a knee-slapper than anything written by Roseanne's favorite funnyman, Samuel Beckett, that existential Yuckmaster General.

Perhaps *Seinfeld* does not elevate the viewer spiritually, as some of the great works of art of the past can claim, but to its credit the show doesn't lie to us either. Larry David's credo for the show—"No learning, no hugging"—may not be an ideal way to live, but it does make for a TV series that doesn't underestimate its audience or rehash the usual comedy clichés. We're talking about a show, after all, in which people are almost as self-absorbed as they are in real life, a show that can breathe new comic life into what might seem like the most stock of characters—such as the wacky next-door neighbor or the disgruntled postman.

It has often been theorized that human beings use only a very small percentage of their brain mass on a regular basis. In everyday terms, this means that despite what the success of *Walker, Texas Ranger* and *Touched by an Angel* might suggest, people are not stupid. For years now, we have proven ourselves up to the challenge of expanding our minds and embracing *Seinfeld,* and that alone is a solid reason for some limited optimism about the state of our society today. As the century draws to its big-bang close without the promise of new adventures from Jerry, George, Elaine and Kramer, the preeminent place of *Seinfeld* in our pop culture is a positive indication that, in the end, perhaps we're not quite as screwed up as the show so artfully and hilariously suggests we are.

SEINING OFF
GEORGE STEINBRENNER on *Seinfeld*

The famed owner of the New York Yankees has played a major role in the Seinfeld *success story without ever actually appearing on-screen. Actually, he did shoot a scene for "The Invitations," but it didn't run for reasons explained best by the man himself. Still, as Steinbrenner makes clear here,* Seinfeld *is still part of the pride of the Yankees.*

Did you ever think you were going to become a sitcom star?

No. There are those people that think I'm a sitcom but not a star.

What went through your head when Jerry Seinfeld asked permission to make you a character?

Well, I've done a number of things before. I did *Saturday Night Live* and I had a lot of fun being the host, and I did a sitcom starring Ryan O'Neal and Farrah Fawcett, you know, single episodes.

But did any of those shows have the impact of Seinfeld*?*

Well no, because *Seinfeld*'s the number one show in the country, I guess.

So has Seinfeld *been good for the Yankees?*

If you can't laugh at yourself in life you're in pretty bad shape. I don't think it's hurt. As long as

Damn Yankees: George hard at work with Bronx Bomber Danny Tartabul.

they don't smear the Yankees—and I don't think they can—I don't mind a little good-natured poking at me. More people—including my own grandchildren—they think nothing of the Yankees or the few other accomplishments in my lifetime. The only thing they care about is "Bubba, you on *Seinfeld*!"

You actually filmed a guest spot that never appeared. What was that like?

I was tremendously impressed by them. I went out to shoot some commercials for the all-star game, George Costanza and I shot them. While I was out there they said, "Why don't we shoot an episode?" It turns out that Elaine's father was a classmate of mine at Culver, a military academy I went to in Indiana. So right away, I had an in there. These kids are so talented—they wing it. You're not always reading a script. We did a scene—a cute scene—but then they changed that episode to have the girl George is going to marry die licking the envelopes. I said, "Put me on the cutting room floor, I don't want any part of that. That's *sick*." But they are *so* talented.

Did you ever get an opportunity to speak with Larry David about the way he does your voice?

I talked to him out there—I think he's one of the fellows I talked to.

Do you think David's impression captures something about you?

He captures a few things about me, and I think maybe they portray me a little too accurately. They portray everything very accurate—from the parking lot to all the office stuff. And we have a fellow who works for me in Tampa, who looks and acts *exactly* like Costanza.

In the last season, George left the Yankees—will you miss him in the front office?

Well, I hope he comes back—these guys always do. They leave in a fit of anger, but they always come back to the Yankee organization.

Any favorite Seinfeld *characters?*

Oh, they're all so good. Naturally, Costanza is the closest to me. He's an *outstanding* young man. But they're all so talented and nice. They've been nice to include us.

So then it's fair to say you're proud to be part of the Seinfeld *legacy?*

Well, I'm happy that I'm part of this particular legend, because I think that's what *Seinfeld* will become on TV.

Pilot Error: George meets his sitcom doppelgänger in "The Pilot," part of *Seinfeld*'s bad-show-within-a-great-show subplot.

YADA YADA

A NOT-SO-SHORT HISTORY OF *SEINFELD*

Though it barely seems worth re-marking upon, a close look at the entirety of recorded human history undertaken in the preparation of this book suggests fairly convincingly that there *was* in fact a world before *Seinfeld*. In reality, it only *seems* as though creation began with the very first entrance of Kramer. For me, all of those long dog days between *Beowulf* and the broadcast of the initial *Seinfeld Chronicles* pilot can now be looked back on as a sort of creative Dark Ages.

In the beginning, there were the heavens and the earth, and more important for our higher purposes here, there was the slightly unlikely partnership of Jerry Seinfeld and Larry David. These yin and yang masters, who together forged the *Seinfeld* sensibility, first met in the comedy clubs of New York City in the mid-seventies. Though David was seven years older than Seinfeld, it would be fair to say that Seinfeld's career was going a bit more smoothly at the time, as evidenced by the fact that NBC was at least mod-estly interested in doing some funny business with him. Apparently the net-work wanted to keep a talent like Sein-feld off any competing network's late-night schedule, and in the mean-time they were willing to throw a few bucks at him by giving him a shot at making a sitcom pilot.

NBC certainly had good reason to be interested in doing more than lunch with the comedian. Without any flashy gimmicks or self-conscious edginess, Seinfeld had established himself as a headlining standout stand-up comic on the then-well-traveled yuck-it-up-for-a-cover-and-two-drink-minimum cir-cuit. In a world of self-consciously stoned would-be rebels and shock effect novelty acts, Seinfeld stood apart by virtue of an approach that was under-stated and observational, yet thoroughly unpretentious. Seinfeld's comedic terri-tory was on the edges of the main-stream; he demonstrated a unique ability to score big with observations of the minute and the obscure. His sensibility was not self-consciously cool in any obvious way, and thus eminently cool. As Seinfeld told Bill Zehme in the September 1994 issue of *Esquire,* "I don't think I'm hip. I'm like in the hip sidecar."

Baby boomer Jerry Seinfeld was born in Brooklyn, New York, on April 29, 1954. He had grown up on Long Island, and even attended high school in Massapequa (which he has joked is Indian for "by the mall") with the tacky embodiment of the region, onetime Amy Fisher paramour Joey Buttafuoco. Seinfeld's immediate family consisted of mother Betty, sister Carolyn and father Kalman, who died in 1985. Seinfeld senior ran the Kal Signfeld Sign Co., a sign painting business.

A comedy buff from an early age, Jerry attended Queens College, where he majored in theater arts and mass communications and graduated in 1976. On his graduation day, Seinfeld celebrated by taking the subway to his first gig onstage at Catch a Rising Star, a famed New York comedy club. In the fall of 1979, Seinfeld gave up waiting at Brew and Burger on the East Side and started emceeing at the Comic Strip two nights a week, earning $70 a week for his trouble. But Seinfeld was too much of a crowd pleaser to struggle long, and he was soon a star on the circuit.

His brilliant friend Larry David, on the other hand, was a cult favorite whose cult consisted of a rather high percentage of other comedians as opposed to, say, a tremendous mass of actual paying customers. David was perhaps best known for his brilliant self-destructive way of berating the audience and himself from the stage—certainly a brave and provocative practice in a strict Brechtian sense, but hardly the sort of approach likely to make one a favorite at less-than-arty laugh factories of the time, which inevitably had names like Laffs or Mister Giggles.

To some this might make David seem like a surprising match for Seinfeld, whose stand-up was more conventionally congenial, but as he told Mark Morrison in *US* magazine in 1992, "My sense of humor offstage is usually kind of raw and antisocial." Compared to Seinfeld, David also brought consider-

GREAT DATES IN *SEINFELD* HISTORY— A HIGHLY SELECTIVE TIME LINE

What follows is a highly ambitious and inaccurate time line dating from the days of the dinosaurs to the age of the Soup Nazi. These are just some of the key events that have helped make the world of *Seinfeld* the beautiful mess that it is. Think of this section as a learned search to place *Seinfeld* in its proper and fitting historical context.

able previous TV experience to the table, having gotten paid to write for NBC's famed *Saturday Night Live* as well as both writing and appearing on the low-rated *Saturday Night Live* retread known as *Fridays,* an ABC show that ran from 1980 to 1982, when ABC decided it would be more profitable to add another night of *Nightline* to the schedule instead.

Still, David has pointed out that it was NBC's interest in Seinfeld that made all things possible. "Well, obviously I was very fortunate to hook up with Jerry in the first place," David once told *Laugh Factory* magazine. "Believe me, if I had gone to NBC on my own, with an idea, say, about a blind deli man, I don't think you'd be interviewing me."

Appropriately, the original brainstorming for the inspired, over-caffeinated comedy of *Seinfeld* is said to have been hashed out over coffee not at Monk's—the leading fictional food spot on *Seinfeld*—but rather at the Westway Diner at Ninth and Forty-fourth Street in the spring of 1988. On a certain level, the notion for the show was neither especially earth-shattering nor revolutionary. Indeed, as has often been pointed out, the characters of *Seinfeld* were not created out of whole neurotic cloth, but rather were based partly on some real-life figures. "Jerry was the only one that was created," Larry David joked to the audience attending an evening honoring *Seinfeld* at the Museum of Television and Radio in 1992.

Despite David's wonderfully ironic wisecrack, the consensus has long been that the character of Jerry Seinfeld was based in large part on . . . Jerry Seinfeld. George Costanza is said to share at least a few characteristics with Larry David. Back in 1993, Larry Charles, one of the greatest *Seinfeld* writers, confessed to Bill Zehme in *Rolling Stone,* "George is Larry David's id. He embodies all the dark impulses that Larry David has occasionally acted upon." The world's worst-kept secret, meanwhile, was that Kramer—later to be revealed as Cosmo Kramer—was based on one Kenny Kramer, David's own idiosyncratic neighbor who now runs and zealously promotes an entertaining *Seinfeld*-related Manhattan tour.

10 to 20 billion B.C.: The Big Bang occurs, theoretically speaking.

1 million B.C.: The setting for an early Raquel Welch movie of the same name. Welch will reemerge many centuries later—looking just a few weeks older—in "The Summer of George," the final episode of the 1996–1997 season.

2 million B.C.: The Big Salad is served to cave dwellers who complain about the service.

5000 B.C.: The first dinosaur walks the earth.

4999 B.C.: A dinosaur with funny hair, known as the K-Rex, makes the first wacky entrance through his neighbor's doorway.

As for Elaine Benes—a character who did not appear in the original *Seinfeld Chronicles* pilot but was soon added—she was said to have been informed by a number of women whom Seinfeld and David had known, including Carol Leifer, a veteran comedienne, onetime Jerry Seinfeld paramour and eventual *Seinfeld* scribe who's gone on to star in her own charming, vaguely *Seinfeld*-esque WB series, *Alright, Already*. This sort of limited crossover between *Seinfeld* and reality was not by any means entirely unprecedented—think of the wildly inventive *Burns and Allen Show*, which broke "the third wall" back in the fifties, or the similarly wall-busting *It's Garry Shandling's Show*, which made a splash in the late eighties and helped set the stage for Shandling's own later nineties masterpiece, *The Larry Sanders Show*.

NO LEARNING, NO HUGGING

The sitcom that Seinfeld and David dreamt up together would be significantly defined not just by what it was, but also by what it was *not*. Recent TV history, after all, is littered with the corpses of comedians who have been slotted into situation comedies with varying degrees of ineffectiveness simply by taking on a different last name, some more conventional career identification, and throwing some half-baked half hour of hijinks at the American public. Many of these shows ended up offering more situation than actual comedy and were thankfully short-lived. *The Bob Newhart Show* was one brilliant early exception to what has become a rather rotten programming rule. (On the other hand, take a show like the unfortunately titled *Platypus Man*, a less than tasty 1995 UPN series in which the talented stand-up comic Richard Jeni played a cooking-show host. Please.)

Thankfully, *Seinfeld* would not become just another highly contrived "feel-good" piece of TV comedy schlock that actually felt *bad* for anyone having to sit and watch it. In a cannibalistic genre where copycat creations are epidemic, *Seinfeld* would make it a point of pride to go its own way. As Seinfeld told

4500 B.C.: The first cave drawings of a Newman-like figure appear.

c. 400 B.C.: Plato passes on the conviction that "the life which is unexamined is not worth living." Since 1989, Jerry, George, Elaine and Cosmo have examined virtually everything.

4000 B.C.: The Bronze Age begins. The wheel is used, as it will be later by George and the gang for drives to suburban malls.

25 B.C.: Sol, the first chatty rabbi, is exiled from Jerusalem.

Glenn Collins in the *New York Times,* the goal was "to do a show where, well, you don't care where it goes. At all. As long as it doesn't go where you think it's going to go."

Larry David's famous credo for the show—"No learning, no hugging"— was more than simply a great throwaway interview line. This was a vaguely revolutionary philosophy that represented a seriously funny and darkly postmodern break from TV funny business as usual. Traditionally, sitcoms had used sentimentality and the illusion of emotional growth as a fallback position once the laughter stopped. *Seinfeld* avoided such a hokey contrivance with a vengeance. "It is a bit presumptuous to think that you can really teach people a meaningful lesson after twenty-one minutes of bad one-liners and to try to get philosophical in that last minute and have it hit home," David explained to *Rolling Stone*'s Fred Schruers in 1994.

Certainly, *Seinfeld* did not invent the notion of having an edge. In a 1997 article in the *New York Review of Books,* Geoffrey O'Brien rightly pointed out that the emotional tone of *Seinfeld* "is a throwback to the frank mutual aggressiveness of Laurel and Hardy or Abbott and Costello." Certainly, Sergeant Bilko was a manipulative and self-serving liar decades before George Costanza made a veritable art form of such bad behavior, but *Seinfeld* was still daring in its willingness to fully embrace its own highly evolved emotional immaturity.

Seinfeld created a one-of-a-kind dysfunction junction, a place where everybody knows not only your name but also all your bizarre neurotic eccentricities. This would be a show about a bunch of thirtysomethings—with maybe even a fortysomething thrown in there—who remain perennially adolescent, wallowing in their infantile yet postsexual lifestyle. In this sense—and likely only in this sense—the world of *Seinfeld* is not unlike that of *Melrose Place,* the popular, soapy prime-time drama of the nineties that Jerry ultimately confesses to watching in "The Beard."

The closest thing to love that we see these characters sharing is a sort of mutual tolerance. What other viable

0: Jesus—a.k.a. Jesus Christ—is born. Eventually, George will do some groundbreaking work on the phenomenon known as the Christ complex.

A.D. 500 to 1000: The Dark Ages, thus named because *Seinfeld* was not yet available in syndication.

Fifth century A.D.: Attila the Hun overruns much of Europe. In the fall of 1992, Elaine will tour the same continent with Dr. Reston, her strange boyfriend and shrink. In the summer of 1997, she will again overrun the continent with boyfriend Dave Puddy.

c. 1310: Dante Alighieri writes *The Divine Comedy.*
c. 1992: Larry David writes perhaps the most divine *Seinfeld* episode, "The Contest."

explanation is there for why, for example, a control freak like Jerry has left open his door to Kramer, rather than—as might happen in real life—locking the door and possibly pressing criminal charges.

Lest you think this author is being far in the September 16, 1996, issue of the *New York Observer*. "Horrible, despicable human beings. But we see there's a little of us in them, our own dark character."

The *Seinfeld* actors too have felt free to join in on this inter-*Seinfeld* character

> "These are the most shallow, superficial, self-indulgent people—people who mug old ladies, burn down log cabins, break up other couples. Horrible, despicable human beings. But we see there's a little of us in them, our own dark character."
>
> —*Larry David to the* New York Observer

too harsh on our beloved *Seinfeld* characters, consider that the creators of the series have themselves appeared to take considerable delight in bad-mouthing the moral stature of their own famous creations. "These are the most shallow, superficial, self-indulgent people—people who mug old ladies, burn down log cabins, break up other couples, think about it," Larry David told Jim Windolf bashing. "The reality is that these four characters are a pathetic group," Julia Louis-Dreyfus told *Rolling Stone*, "and they should disassemble promptly. I mean, if you stand back from it and look at what happens every week, they do *terrible* things to one another. And yet they continue to hang out. It's sociopathic. It's nuts! This is a sick group of people."

If Sigmund Freud—one *very* funny

c. 1387: Geoffrey Chaucer's *The Canterbury Tales* includes the line, "Each man for himself"—an attitude that prevails on the *Seinfeld* tales to this very day.

1532: Machiavelli's *The Prince* defines a certain sort of ruthless behavior. In 1989, *Seinfeld* elaborates on the personal politics of selfishness.

German fellow, incidentally, and a man who knew a thing or two about sick people—was correct in his "release theory" from *Jokes and Their Relation to the Unconscious* that humor provides us with a relatively healthy outlet for repressed sexual or aggressive impulses, then perhaps the intelligent darkness that has come to mark the *Seinfeld* worldview might actually represent a sort of humorous safety valve that can save our collective asses. In other words, it's possible that the *Seinfeld* gang dysfunctions weekly not only so that we can get a few inexpensive laughs, but also so that we might not have to be quite as screwed up as those folks acting out on-screen.

Make that screwed up but incredibly smart folks. *Seinfeld* has explored what might be termed the comedy of thinking persons' stasis. Indeed, much of the humor of *Seinfeld* could be called gallows humor set in the realm of highly intelligent people trying to find stupid ways to kill time together. And as Miguel de Unamuno once wrote, "Killing time is perhaps the essence of comedy." But right from his decision to bring a dark comedy

knight like Larry David into his brave comedy quest, it was clear that Jerry Seinfeld wasn't looking to simply kill airtime with the usual clichés. *Seinfeld* redefined what the mainstream could be by having a substantial portion of America—and eventually the planet— marching to the offbeat. As Seinfeld told *Playboy*'s David Rensin in 1993, "Almost everything we do is about being offbeat. Even ordinary things somehow come out offbeat. We don't want to do stuff we've seen."

Seinfeld was envisioned with enough foresight that it wouldn't be just another runaway comedy train on the laugh track to absolutely nowhere. The show would in certain ways try to tell the truth, a sort of truth one didn't generally get from those Olsen twins on *Full House*.

"I wanted to do a show about being a comedian," Seinfeld told comedy great Alan King, then host of Comedy Central's *Inside the Comedy Mind* series. "I didn't want to just play Skippy the wacky neighbor."

Part of the reason Jerry Seinfeld may have felt this way could be viewed as

1813: In *Pride and Prejudice*, Jane Austen writes, "For what do we live, but to make sport for our neighbors, and laugh at them in our turn?" These wise words from a red-hot author will later prove invaluable in helping to make sense and sensibility of why Jerry and Kramer spend so much damn time with each other.

1844: Friedrich Wilhelm Nietzsche is born. He will go on to write *Thus Spake Zarathustra*, which explains his concept of the Superman. A century later, Jerry will go public with his own fascination with Superman.

quite pragmatic. For all his other plentiful and rare virtues, Seinfeld is certainly no classically trained master thespian. Though the record shows he had already been cast as Frankie, the governor's joke writer and/or messenger, on *Benson,* he lost that job after just a few guest shots back in 1980. A brilliant comic, a writer and producer of enduring excellence—and clearly the very best person alive to play the role of Jerry Seinfeld—he was still at the time no great shakes as an actor. His main strength and appeal in this regard could be seen in his ability to come across like the smart-ass next door. "I have no hook," he explained insightfully to Alan King. "I'm not the guy that . . . I'm *that* guy." To his credit, Jerry Seinfeld—one of the funniest men alive—was ready and willing to play a relative straight man to some even more messed-up characters.

In the *Seinfeld* casting process, "that guy" was effectively surrounded by an impressive cast that featured prodigious amounts of both acting experience and talent. Seinfeld wisely placed himself in a context where he was learning by

doing and rising to the hilarious occasion. We'd see him doing some stand-up and then see him in his "natural" environment. As a rule, Seinfeld was still not called on to stretch too far—as Larry David told Schruers, "We try to keep Jerry and Jerry as close as we can. We don't want him to do too much acting." In "The Pilot"—one of the series of *Seinfeld* episodes that share the absurdity of the sitcom-building process—Jerry tells Kramer, who is suddenly desperate to play himself, "Why do we need two people in the cast who can't act?"

Right from the beginning, *Seinfeld* would savvily avoid such a talent problem by supporting Seinfeld with a cast of awesome comic abilities. Indeed, as Julia Louis-Dreyfus told Steve Kroft of *60 Minutes* in 1996 with her tongue apparently only mildly in cheek, "The focus is really the three of us." In speaking to Kroft, Larry David also was quick to credit the fundamental charm and skill of the cast with helping make the darkness of the material on *Seinfeld* so palatable: "This material in the hands of other actors . . . the show would be a disaster."

1856: Sigmund Freud is born. Along with pioneering his highly influential psychoanalytic method, he is credited with saying "Sometimes a cigar is just a cigar." In 1992, cigar enthusiast Kramer—a man who might baffle even Freud himself—will burn down Mr. Ross's cabin with some Cubans.

1865: Actor John Wilkes Booth assassinates President Abraham Lincoln at the Ford Theater, proclaiming "Sic Semper Tyrannis"—meaning "Thus Always to Tyrants." Almost 130 years later, Crazy Joe Davola offers the same words as he interrupts the filming of the first and only episode of *Jerry*.

For this reason the *Seinfeld* casting process—supervised by the show's casting director Marc Hirshfeld—was a major turning point for the show. Even with an ambitious concept and groundbreaking writing, *Seinfeld* needed one more key element: the exact right people for the gig of a lifetime.

WHO *ARE* THESE PEOPLE?

The first cast—after Jerry Seinfeld, of course—was Jason Alexander, an apparently natural-born actor who began his life as Jay Scott Greenspan on September 23, 1959. Growing up in the New Jersey towns of Maplewood and Livingston, the son of a father in manufacturing and a mom in nursing, Alexander sang and acted his way through Livingston High School. He went on to win a drama scholarship to Boston University, but dropped out when he got his first small—and I do mean *small*—break by scoring a role in a low-rent and appropriately campy 1981 slasher/summer camp flick entitled *The Burning*.

Alexander had better luck in terms of material for the stage, appearing in Stephen Sondheim's short-lived musical *Merrily We Roll Along* before moving on to more extended runs in Neil Simon's *Broadway Bound* and *Jerome Robbins' Broadway*, for which he received a Tony as Best Actor in a Musical the very year he signed on for what would become extended George duty when he was cast for the *Seinfeld Chronicles* pilot.

Next came Michael Richards, a veteran comic character actor whose abilities Larry David had a chance to get familiar with during the *Fridays* era, since both of them were members of the show's cast. Richards was born in Los Angeles on July 14, 1950, an only child whose electrical engineer father died when he was two. He was raised by his mother, a medical librarian, and apparently demonstrated his extraordinary gifts for physical comedy from an early age. As Richards told the press after winning his third Emmy in 1997, "Ever since I was little, I was crashing my bicycle into a tree to make kids laugh."

The young, Red Skelton–loving bike

1877: A key year for television, as M. Senlecq invents a device known as the "Telectroscope"—a crude sort of television. This will not be the last time that the words "crude" and "television" appear in the same sentence.

1935: Great American humorist Will Rogers—who famously spoke of never meeting a man he didn't like—dies. But then, he never met *Newman*.

1912: Economist Milton Friedman is born. He will later be credited with the phrase, "There is no such thing as a free lunch." In 1994, Elaine will prove Uncle Miltie wrong as she gets a free lunch in "The Big Salad."

The Naked Truth: In or out of the tub, Michael Richards remains one totally hot physical comedian.

1941: On July 1, commercial television service starts. The first licensed station is WNBT, an NBC station. Less than half a century later, NBC will finally get the bugs out of the system and start broadcasting *Seinfeld*.

1944: Jean-Paul Sartre publishes his play *No Exit*, which includes the memorable line "Hell is—other people!" *Seinfeld* will repeatedly confirm this existential point of view.

1950: The Korean War begins. War hero Frank Costanza serves his country with a skillet.

crasher went on to attend Thousand Oaks High School and Los Angeles Valley College and graduated from California Institute of Arts, where he apparently studied holistic phenomenology. After a stint in the army as a medic stationed in West Germany, he moved to San Diego, where he worked with the San Diego Repertory Company. With the eighties looming, he began doing stand-up comedy and popped up often in film and television roles, but Richards had long been a brilliant comic actor waiting for a forum worthy of his remarkable abilities. As Seinfeld told *Playboy,* "Michael Richards has a unique talent, which needed to find a place. Before the show nobody was using him properly." Let this much be said for *Seinfeld*—they sure know how to use people.

Last but not least came the most fetching member of the *Seinfeld* fab four. Julia Louis-Dreyfus was born in New York City on January 13, 1961. Because her parents split when she was very young, she grew up dividing her time between the New York State home of her father—a businessman and lawyer who ran the family's successful arbitrage firm—and the Washington, D.C., area home of her mother, a writer. Both parents remarried, and young Louis-Dreyfus even spent one year in Sri Lanka with her mother and stepfather, a surgeon who was then working for an international relief organization. The president of the drama club at Holton-Arms, a swanky all-girls high school in Bethesda, Maryland, Louis-Dreyfus went on to study theater at Northwestern University in Illinois, where she became involved with the Practical Theater, an improv group, as well as Chicago's better-known Second City company. She also became involved with her eventual husband, Brad Hall, who was part of the Practical Theater troupe.

Before Louis-Dreyfus could graduate from Northwestern, she and Hall were recruited to join the cast of *Saturday Night Live*. There Louis-Dreyfus met Larry David, who was in the midst of what was by most accounts one highly unproductive season with the show. Louis-Dreyfus lasted longer than David,

1961: John F. Kennedy is elected president of the United States of America. In his inaugural address, Kennedy proclaimed, "Let us never negotiate out of fear, but let us never fear to negotiate." This may have influenced the *Seinfeld* cast's high profile in courage during the 1997 contract negotiations.

1980: The "Who Shot J.R.?" issue explodes into the public consciousness on the March 21 episode of *Dallas*. Years later absolutely no one will wonder who killed Susan on *Seinfeld*.

July 5, 1989: *The Seinfeld Chronicles* airs—millions fail to take notice. This initial low-rated late-eighties airing achieves little other than to assure that deep-thinking writers are not entirely correct when they call *Seinfeld* the show of the nineties.

toiling there from 1982 to 1985, but she too has spoken of feeling somewhat lost on *Saturday Night Live* despite having made a small splash spoofing everyone from MTV VJ Nina Blackwood to Marie Osmond. "It was competitive, very male-oriented," she told Melinda Gerosa in an October 1997 cover story in *Ladies' Home Journal.* "It wasn't *fun.*"

Louis-Dreyfus has said she was happier during two seasons on the forgettable late-eighties NBC sitcom *Day by Day.* Still, her TV work and appearances in assorted films from *Hannah and Her Sisters* to *Troll* rarely gave her a chance to show off her considerable chops. Amazed by Elaine's ability to fake an orgasm in "The Mango," Jerry Seinfeld says of Elaine, "She's like Meryl Streep, this woman." The comment applies to Louis-Dreyfus as well—not that Louis-Dreyfus and Elaine Benes are one and the same. As Jerry Seinfeld told *US* magazine's Josh Rottenberg in 1997, "Julia's got it together, and Elaine's a mess."

To hear the players tell it, the chemistry between the cast members was almost instantaneous. Asked during an interview by Los Angeles radio personality Michael Jackson about how long it took for the ensemble to coalesce, Jason Alexander explained, "I think it happened within weeks of beginning, when we just started enjoying each other so much. . . . We didn't think it would catch on, so we just started enjoying each other and supporting each other, and before you knew it we had an amazing ensemble."

KEEPING HOPE ALIVE

Even with all that talent both in front of and behind the camera, *Seinfeld* remains a pop-cultural phenomenon that very nearly wasn't. *The Seinfeld Chronicles*—dumped on the air on July 5, 1989, amid the summer reruns—was basically a failed pilot. And unbelievably, that almost certainly would have been the end of that if Rick Ludwin, an NBC vice president of late night, variety and specials, had not fought the good fight and somehow

May 31, 1990: The world meets Elaine in "The Stakeout."

January 29, 1992: Everyone says "Hello, Newman" as Wayne Knight is seen on *Seinfeld* for the first time.

November 18, 1992: "The Contest" airs—later that night, masturbation becomes all the rage in America.

convinced then-president Brandon Tartikoff to do four more episodes that would air the following summer. At a 1992 appearance at the Museum of Television and Radio, Seinfeld saluted Ludwin as "the one responsible for the show being on the air."

As for Tartikoff, Seinfeld was one of the many TV greats who attended the late, great executive's funeral in 1997, and saluted him publicly. Fondly, Seinfeld recalled how Tartikoff had expressed his worries about the show, namely, that "it's too New York, it's too Jewish." But Seinfeld still gave Tartikoff credit for ultimately opting to give the show its big shot despite such misgivings.

Seinfeld and David benefited from having Castle Rock involved as a production entity in the creation of the show. Previously Seinfeld had met with Castle Rock about starring in a show called *Past Imperfect* which ended up proceeding, albeit briefly, with Howie Mandel. In 1995, Seinfeld told David Kronke in the *Los Angeles Times*, "NBC has been terrific with us, but Castle Rock is the one who really made the show. They put up the money, they ran interference, they developed the whole idea. Castle Rock is responsible for the look of the show, the quality. I wanted it on film, which is very expensive—no one else would have given me that."

Certainly, the industry wasn't exactly abuzz about the show in the beginning. The *Seinfeld Chronicles* pilot episode—written by David and Seinfeld, and directed by Art Wolff—was reviewed on July 3, 1989, by *Daily Variety* critic Tony Scott, who wrote: "The format's agreeable enough," but despite granting quite correctly that the show had "promise," his praise seemed halfhearted, with a clear suggestion of the show being highly derivative: "The Garry Shandling blueprint comes to mind, since *Seinfeld* is a watered-down version."

NBC's own research was, to put it kindly, less than entirely encouraging. Over the years, Jerry Seinfeld has taken considerable pleasure in reading the original research report to reporters. For instance, he told Kronke, "The report was really bad. It just said, 'Jerry needs a

September 23, 1993: Jerry dons the Puffy Shirt. Thankfully, he fails to start a fashion trend.

September 21, 1995: George proposes to Susan. Hell fails to freeze over.

January 5, 1995: Humanitarians Jerry and George make one giant step for mankind when they hash out a way to pull off The Great Roommate Switch.

stronger supporting cast,' 'It's hard to get excited about two guys going to the laundromat,' 'Jerry is dense and indecisive,' 'Why are they interrupting the stand-up for these stupid stories?'"

The network's minuscule vote of confidence early on seems to have stuck ever so slightly in Seinfeld's craw. Years later in 1996, Jerry Seinfeld recounted for *60 Minutes'* Steve Kroft how NBC had ordered only four new shows, "which is the smallest number of episodes ever ordered by a network. . . . Four. I mean, six is a slap in the face."

This particular slap in the face also served as a crucial, if temporary, stay of execution for the show. NBC's short run of the retooled series—now called *Seinfeld*—aired in May and June of 1990. By May 31, 1990, in reviewing the first of these new episodes, "The Stakeout," *Variety's* Tony Scott mentioned the show's "gentle humor, sometimes pointed but never hurtful. . . . If the word 'bland' comes to mind, it's because sitcoms aren't usually understated."

Bland would not be a word often used to describe the show, which would increasingly take on a distinctively negative, inside, New Yawkish tone, one arguably too distinctive for its own commercial good. Seinfeld and David must have known on some level such concerns might be entirely reasonable, at least according to the sort of demographic thinking that runs rampant in TV circles. Fortunately, such limited thought proves useless in relation to popular art of enduring value. No doubt some publisher probably thought Joyce's *Ulysses* was "too Dublin."

During the 1992 tribute to *Seinfeld* at the Museum of Television and Radio, Jerry Seinfeld addressed this issue. He explained his own sense that audiences like something better if they believe that it sounds authentic, "even if they don't get it, you know. There's nothing worse than feeling something's been homogenized so we can *all* understand it."

On *Seinfeld,* the comedy would be far from homogenized. This is a show, after all, in which high and low culture collide exquisitely. What other show would dare throw a Leopold and Loeb reference into an episode called "The Junior

September 25, 1997: Newman grapples with the temptation of cannibalism—another comedy taboo is chewed up and spit out by *Seinfeld*.

May 16, 1996: Susan Biddle Ross dies in "The Invitations"—a rare TV death played entirely for laughs. Hey, it could have been worse: She could have lived and tried to sustain a marriage with George. Also the last episode before Larry David moved on.

May 14, 1998: The end of the world as we know it (and we won't feel fine).

MATCHMAKERS, MATCHMAKERS

As you might do at "The Chinese Restaurant," match one from column A with one from column B.

1. Golda Meir	a. The real Jerry Seinfeld's birthday
2. $1.3 million	b. The high price for a thirty-second ad spot during the Super Bowl
3. April 29	c. Newman's New Year's Eve booking for the millennium
4. Leonid Brezhnev	d. Jerry's choice for least attractive world leader
5. DeSoto	e. Jason Alexander's birthday
6. Christopher Cross	f. Kramer's audition stage name for "The Pilot"
7. $2 million	g. Jerry's favorite explorer
8. September 23	h. Elaine's choice for least attractive world leader
9. Martin Van Nostrum	i. George's favorite explorer
10. Magellan	j. The high price for a thirty-second ad spot during the *Seinfeld* season finale

Mint"? As its audience came to take these idiosyncrasies to heart, *Seinfeld* grew to become a show that played with and detonated conventions, thus breaking with many of the doggedly Pavlovian expectations of the sitcom genre.

Ironically, *Seinfeld* brought a strange sense of reality to situation comedy—the truth of the matter is that in real life people *are* this screwed up, yet somehow lovable. On the show, comedy of the darkest and lightest shades plays off each other to brilliant effect. This duality explains the warmly sadomasochistic quality that makes *Seinfeld*—as the great *Washington Post* TV critic Tom Shales once gracefully put it—"painfully amusing and amusingly painful."

However amusing it was, in the context of the high-stakes crapshoot that is contemporary TV, where shows are rarely given a plethora of chances to connect, it still took a considerable amount of time for *Seinfeld* to be understood by a mass audience. NBC may not have been entirely sure what the hell to do with *Seinfeld*, but to its eternal artistic and fiscal credit, the network nonetheless

SEINING OFF
JUDGE REINHOLD on *Seinfeld*

The film actor perhaps best known for his hysterical work in the Beverly Hills Cop *films,
Reinhold was deservedly Emmy-nominated as Outstanding Guest Actor in a Comedy Series for his
hilarious, in-your-face role as Aaron the Close Talker in "The Raincoats" episode of* Seinfeld.
Way before that, we discover here, he was an early Michael Richards booster.

The comic circumstances of that episode were so great, I really honestly felt *that's* what I was hon-
ored for, because I've worked a lot harder other times without getting that sort of notoriety. What
was funny was that it was the great comic actor Martin Sheen who won that year. I was up against
Paul Dooley, who I greatly admire, and also Jason Alexander and all these comic actors. And Martin Sheen did a *Murphy Brown* and they gave it to him.

As an actor, did you do a lot of investigation into the motivation of the close talker?
I certainly did give it some thought. He's a guy who has no understanding of social boundaries,
he lacks that chip. I watched for a couple weeks how people have an innate respect for boundaries,
and some people need more space than others. I try to be very sensitive to people and it was a little
difficult for me to just invade like that in rehearsal. I think Jerry was a little awkward with it at first.
We laughed a lot, but I *really* had to go nose-to-nose with Jerry.

Was it at all daunting stepping into that ensemble?
I didn't feel that. I knew Michael Richards because we both studied with Stella Adler, who could
not understand Michael *at all*. This was after *Fridays*. He did really fine work in that class. He did a
scene from *Zoo Story* and I remember her saying, "Who *are* you?" I pulled him aside—because he'd
done really great—and I said, "Michael, you're such a contemporary talent, I just don't think she
gets you." And he said, "*Contemporary*, yeah," so then he could go home and sleep. But no, I didn't
feel intimidated. I was nothing but excited. This was one of the greatest ensembles ever in TV and I
was really grateful for the opportunity to work with them. I loved working with Julia—she's *really*
spontaneous. And it was fun to watch them all find their places.

So why was Aaron so interested in spending time with Morty and Helen Seinfeld?
I think it was a paternal thing. He was probably alienated by his own parents.

Do people ever bring up the character of Aaron when they see you?
They *literally* bring it up to me—they come nose-to-nose with me, which is sometimes *extremely*

annoying. It happens all the time, and they say, "Loved you on *Seinfeld*," and they get right in my face. Before they say that, I'm taken aback because they're invading my space.

Perhaps you should stay home the day after reruns?

I've gotten tremendous response from it, and still do. I'm really delighted with it. There's something else about that episode that I heard. The last part of the episode is sort of a satire on *Schindler's List.* Well, when Steven Spielberg was making *Schindler's List*—because it was such a grim, bleak film for him—he ordered all the *Seinfeld*s he could get to watch overseas while he was shooting. So he's a big fan, and we were all a little concerned about what he'd think, but apparently he enjoyed the takeoff.

So who's your favorite Seinfeld *character?*

Well, for me it's a toss-up between Elaine and Kramer. Michael *really* makes me laugh. The first day of rehearsal he wears elbow pads and knee pads because he just doesn't know what he's going to do. He's two hundred percent committed to his work. I love their inventiveness and enjoyed watching them put their own stamp on the material.

kept the show on the air, albeit in some strange and seemingly unnatural time slots. For the fall season beginning in 1991, *Seinfeld* found itself sandwiched between *Night Court* and *Quantum Leap* on Wednesdays at 9:30 P.M. The next fall, *Seinfeld* started the 1992–1993 season at 9:00 P.M. between the inexplicable lead-in *Unsolved Mysteries* and the infinitely more appropriate lead-out *Mad About You.*

Finally, *Seinfeld* got a serious leg-up in the Nielsens by virtue of some close proximity to America's favorite social drinkers—the cast of *Cheers.* It was not until early 1993, when *Seinfeld* was moved from Wednesday to Thursday right after *Cheers,* that the show finally connected in a major way, and in the fall of 1993 *Seinfeld* replaced *Cheers* as the anchor show of what remains a Must See night of television, a position once occupied by Seinfeld's early hero Bill Cosby. Now firmly in the public eye, *Seinfeld* was third in the Nielsens for the 1993–1994 season—and by the next season it leapt to the top of the annual ratings. The show even managed to slay a more mainstream beast in the form of Tim Allen's ABC smash *Home Improvement.* From there the show was well on its way to world domination and the overwhelmingly profitable world of syndication.

All this ado for a show said to be about nothing? In fact, even Seinfeld himself has pointed out that the notion of the show's nothingness is somewhat overblown. As he told the *Hollywood Reporter*'s Rick Sherwood, "Well, nothing and everything are really the same thing." Seinfeld went on to explain that the premise of the show involved looking at "the mini-events of life—the kinds of things that comprise most of life for most people. . . . I call it microcomedy."

In his best-selling book *SeinLanguage*, Jerry Seinfeld writes, "To me the worst thing about television is that everybody you see on television is doing something better than what you're doing. You never see anybody on TV just sliding off the front of the sofa with potato chip crumbs all over their shirt." Part of the beauty of *Seinfeld*—and there's plenty of beauty to go around—is that as we laugh uproariously, we can also actually look down our noses at people whose lives are—staggeringly enough—even more absurd than our own.

WORLD DOMINATION FOR FUN AND PROFIT

Fortuitously, just as the show about nothing was achieving world domination for fun and profit, *Seinfeld* was also hitting its stride creatively speaking. The breakthrough 1993–1994 season featured classic episodes like "The Puffy Shirt," "The Non-Fat Yogurt," "The Conversion" and "The Marine Biologist." While a few of the very early shows have a slightly static and now-dated feel somewhat akin to watching some *Honeymooners* kinescopes, the show gradually found its own visual style and tone under the direction of Tom Cherones and, starting at the beginning of season six, Andy Ackerman. Increasingly, the actors and writers also found the comic centers of the characters, while an equally strong supporting crew of occasional players emerged to offer solid support. *Seinfeld* plots became more and more complex—three plots or more that generally connect at some point. The twenty-two-minute limit actually helps *Seinfeld*—like a haiku, it seems to give a sympathetic form to the show's genius. Indeed, the occasional hourlong episodes rarely double our pleasure.

The show began pushing the envelope in exciting ways. During the winter of 1992, *Seinfeld* delivered back-to-back risqué masterpiece episodes with "The Virgin"—about Jerry dating one—and "The Contest," which grapples with masturbation. *Seinfeld* could get away with such plots only because of the writers' inspired, inventive use of double-talk and innuendo. As Seinfeld told Schruers, "I really enjoy the art of euphemism, especially compared to the shove-it-up-your-nose kind of stuff they usually do on TV."

Beyond the show's increasingly strong writing, the entire *Seinfeld* ensemble demonstrated their own excellent learning curves.

Seinfeld himself, though still not quite the Jewish De Niro, grew ever more confident as an actor. The character of Jerry—seemingly the normal one—started showing his own cold perfectionist streak, which became ever more apparent as his attractive and appealing love interests were dismissed for the

Morrison in September 1992. "With him as the guide, the audience will plunge into depths they might not go into otherwise." Carol Leifer has credited some of Jerry's apparent Teflon appeal to his winning boy-man quality. As she told *Rolling Stone*'s Schruers in 1994, Seinfeld had a quality that made him adorable even when he was being shallow in an episode like 1993's "The

> ## "You never see anybody on TV just sliding off the front of the sofa with potato chip crumbs all over their shirt."
>
> —*Jerry Seinfeld in* Seinlanguage

slightest hygienic mishap or flaw. Some fans of the show have called for Jerry and Elaine to get back together as a couple. Asked about this at the 1992 *Seinfeld* tribute at the Museum of Television and Radio's Ninth Television Festival in Los Angeles, Seinfeld explained that such a move was unlikely. "We are enjoying casting the weekly girlfriend too much," he said. Interestingly, any red-blooded male cannot help but notice that as the show itself got hotter, so too did the character's transitory love interests.

Jerry Seinfeld had a quality that allowed him to capture the affections of the masses. "Jerry's like Rod Serling," Larry Charles told *US* magazine's Mark

Masseuse." As she put it, "I think with another guy it would have come across kind of skeevy. But Jerry's got this quality that just kind of made it kind of innocent and boyish."

Jason Alexander zeroed in on George quickly, unforgettably capturing the tortured and troubled soul of Costanza—arguably the most Jewish Italian character in history, once accurately described by *Newsday* as "the most fully realized schlemiel in the history of television." Geoffrey O'Brien, writing in the *New York Review of Books* in 1997, pointed out that in the character of George, "the classic Woody Allen neurotic persona is cranked to a far more grating level of

Riot Gal: The ever-adorable and always delectable Elaine Benes mixes at Monk's with a familiar friend.

cringing self-abasement." That said, you still gotta love the guy. George, like Jerry and Kramer, even became a sex symbol for some, though in 1996 Alexander dismissed this notion to Darcy Rice in *Orange Coast,* saying that when he hears such talk "I just have to pity society."

Jerry Seinfeld has said that the decision was made to add a major female character because the show initially "lacked estrogen." But in the hands of Louis-Dreyfus, Elaine Benes quickly became more than just a demographic, estrogen-laced throwaway. She was the excitable girl of our dreams—a woman with the grace to make a simple exclamatory phrase like "Get out!" ring out like poetry. Smart, ambitious and lusty with a becoming dab of postfeminist rage, Elaine soon became a *That Girl* for the riot grrrl age—sort of *That Screwed-Up but Still Extremely Adorable Woman.*

No one embraced his oddball character with more crazed conviction than Michael Richards. In *Seinfeld,* Richards, who takes his wildly funny work very seriously, has once and for all found the right canvas on which to create his art. In a 1997 cover story on Richards in *Cigar Aficionado,* John O'Hurley, who plays J. Peterman, told Alysse Minkoff that watching the actor at work on the *Seinfeld* set for the first time "was like watching Baryshnikov choreograph a ballet. Every move, take and line of dialogue—all the zaniness—was carefully

constructed." Indeed, Richards brought almost expressionistic physicality to the role of Kramer, a man perhaps too much in touch with his aging inner child. A fan of Charlie Chaplin, Buster Keaton and Peter Sellers, Richards said to *US*'s Chris Hamilton in 1992, "I like to do things that are funny rather than say things that are funny."

Soon awards of every sort were coming *Seinfeld*'s way. In 1993, the show won the Emmy for Outstanding Comedy Series, and that same year Richards won as Outstanding Supporting Actor in a Comedy Series for the first time. There would be many more laurels to come. Notably, the show also won a 1992 George Foster Peabody Broadcasting Award, citing the fact that *Seinfeld*'s "comedy is universal and instructive in many aspects of everyday life."

Along with the awards and acclaim came another sort of notoriety, including the attention from tabloids, much of it focusing on Jerry Seinfeld's romantic relationship with Shoshanna Lonstein, a fetching young woman twenty-one years his junior. Hey, at least Seinfeld was making a concerted effort to stay in touch with the show's younger demographic.

By the mid-nineties, a cultural consensus of sorts was developing that *Seinfeld* represented TV history in the making, that rare, shining show that was influential and, far more important, still funny as hell. As *Bright Lights, Big*

SEINING OFF
RAQUEL WELCH on *Seinfeld*

The famed beauty and screen actress (One Million Years B.C., The Three Musketeers, Bedazzled) *was in typically fine form when she played herself as the "train wreck" star of* Scarsdale Surprise, *the show for which Kramer wrongly received a Tony Award during "The Summer of George," the closing episode of* Seinfeld's *eighth season.*

I thoroughly enjoyed your scary performance in "The Summer of George."

That wasn't a *performance*, that was the real me—couldn't you tell? (*Laughs.*) Oh *God*, can you believe I had the guts to do that? That was so horrific—what a *horrible* character she was.

How did it happen?

Well, it was just totally bizarre because for the longest time I've been saying I'd really like to do the *Seinfeld* show. It's such a cool show—the writing is so great, and the acting is so great. I don't watch too much TV, but this is a really good show. I'm interested in doing series television and doing a comedy character and I thought it would be fun for me to get some experience for that. Then all of a sudden I was signed to do *Victor/Victoria*—I guess that's what precipitated this casting idea that I should play the deadliest diva alive. They called me at like ten o'clock at night and they read me the scene over the phone and they wanted me to be there to shoot it the next afternoon. My manager, Steve, said, "Just listen. It's really funny." So I listened and the scene was hysterical. And the whole setup with Kramer was funny—too rich.

So are you considering going on the road with Scarsdale Surprise?

(*Laughs at generous length.*) No. Isn't that a hysterical title—*Scarsdale Surprise*? They're so good, those *Seinfeld* writers. The whole team is so good—it was just a complete pleasure.

Dueling Divas: Kramer, Tony and *Scarsdale Surprise* Raquel Welch in "The Summer of George."

As a sex symbol yourself, do you view Kramer as a sex symbol?

Yes, I do, I do. I absolutely do. Just like Woody Allen or any other of these crazy funny guys. Michael Richards is definitely a sex symbol, and you know he's a sweetheart, he can be very soft-spoken and quite tender as a person. Jerry told me the way his entrance thing began was that he was late for his cue in one of the earlier episodes and he came sliding in and got all discombobulated and that it was so great they just kept that as the whole modus operandi of his character.

What kind of reaction did you get from the episode?

Amazing. I'm here on Broadway and I'm having a blast doing it. And they start to *dis* me in the New York tabloids, saying I've cut all my pieces to shreds, and I'm going, "They saw fuckin' *Seinfeld*, and now they're trying to make it true. They saw the episode and now they're trying to make it true. I knew this would happen. I knew! Now they're gonna think I'm really like that." Secondly, every night when I left the theater there were a lot of people, and they had the police out on horseback and barricades, and when I'd come out invariably people would yell, "We loved you on *Seinfeld*!"—not everyone in unison—but it was funny to me that here I am doing this whole Broadway turn and the *Seinfeld* thing is still following me around.

Do you have any favorite Seinfeld *character?*

For a long time I think I liked Kramer the best because he's the most outrageous. But then lately I've really started getting into Julia. She's really, really good—it's deceptively simple, what she does, but she's just totally off the wall. She's out there. And I like the fact that Jerry was so attentive when you're working with him. He was very *there* as a producer, and very kind and into it. And I thought that's why the show works: Not only is he talented and clever and has a great team, but he likes it. He *really* likes it.

City novelist Jay McInerney wrote in a 1996 *TV Guide* article, the time had come to seriously consider the fact that *Seinfeld* was possibly the greatest sitcom ever: "Now that half the shows on prime time bear a striking resemblance to the show about Jerry and his friends, it behooves us to honor this *Citizen Kane* of situation comedies, and to propose that it may be—as Ralph Kramden would say—the greatest."

Not everyone was quite so effusive or positive about what *Seinfeld* has wrought and what its success says about us.

Any show that gets as big as *Seinfeld* has will at times endure a bit of backlash. Some critics felt there was a dip after the Emmy-winning 1992–1993 season—writing on-line for *Salon*, Joyce Millman had a little trouble with what she perceived as "the bodily-function-obsessed '94–'95 season." Over the years,

Jerry Seinfeld has come off as unapologetic about any perceived creative dips—and with good reason, since the show's high standards of quality control would be the envy of any other long-running series. "Nobody ever talks about other shows slipping, because they were never anywhere to begin with," Seinfeld told Steve Pond during a 1994 *TV Guide* interview.

Even with the stray dog of an episode, *Seinfeld* was enough of a draw to bring an

platter of *mishagas* and mirth. As Bob Daily put it so well in a 1997 *Playboy* profile of Jason Alexander, "George is us; we are George. *Ich bin ein Costanza.*"

THE HUDDLED MASSES

So who exactly was the audience who added up to make this decidedly strange show such a world-beating smash?

Seinfeld is the first TV series to ever command more than $1 million a minute for advertising—only the Super Bowl could make the same claim. That's only fitting, since *Seinfeld* has now become the Super Bowl of comedy.

intelligent, disenfranchised silent majority back to the tube in a time when the networks have been fighting a losing battle to keep up a market share that is disappearing because of cable and apathy. Asked by Darcy Rice, in a 1996 *Orange Coast* cover story, about America's fascination with the characters, Jason Alexander responded, "It just yells to me that people have way, way too much time on their hands." Yet for whatever reasons, many of us do relate in an intimate way to *Seinfeld*'s tasty combo

"The bored, the disaffected, the disenfranchised. The tired, the huddled masses," Seinfeld joked to *Playboy*'s Rensin, and that sounds like just about the right formula for a new fin de siècle mainstream.

Many pop culture pundits have searched for greater societal meaning for the success of the show, beyond the obvious fact that it was substantially funnier than other programming options like *Coach.* A common, relatively reasonable theory was that *Seinfeld*—like most sitcoms—offered a sense of family, albeit a misfit family. Writing in the December 1992 issue of the *Atlantic*, Frances Davis pointed out that the Upper West Side coffee shop hangout where the gang commonly congregates "is the equivalent of the family dinner table in *Father Knows Best* or *Leave It to Beaver* for Seinfeld and his surrogate family of thirtysomethings."

Soon this particular screwed-up family seemed to be spawning everywhere on the tube. Possibly the first show to reflect the *Seinfeld* influence was *Mad About You*, the fine series that debuted in the fall of 1992 starring stand-up Paul Reiser and Helen Hunt as a married couple in Manhattan, which suggested a sort of better-adjusted *Seinfeld* populated with at least a couple of people who could actually commit. Sadly, Hollywood, being the sort of bandwagon-jumping town it is, would start handing out sitcom deals to scores of other comedians with far lesser talents than Jerry Seinfeld, a trend that continues to this day. One happy exception has been *Everybody Loves Raymond*, a charming family sitcom that answers the question: What if Jerry Seinfeld were an Italian sportswriter with a wife and kids? Furthermore, if one agrees that *Friends*—which debuted in the fall of 1994—could be viewed as a twentysomething *Seinfeld* with more obvious sex appeal, then all of the many *Friends* rip-offs were also by extension *Seinfeld* rip-offs as well.

With big influence and big ratings came—you guessed it—big money. One huge payoff came in September 1995, when the first 110 *Seinfeld* episodes began to be syndicated through Columbia TriStar to a record 224 stations at a reported price tag of $3 million per episode. In a 1997 *Business Week* cover story, Elizabeth Lesly reported that *Seinfeld* is the first TV series to ever command more than $1 million a minute for advertising—only the Super Bowl could make the same claim. That's only fitting, since *Seinfeld* has now become the Super Bowl of comedy.

Furthermore, the *Seinfeld* stars started popping up as pitchmen for a wide range of products. The overwhelming goodwill felt toward *Seinfeld*'s stars proved helpful in selling everything from credit cards to pretzels. And don't forget all the movie parts that squeezed in during hiatus. Interestingly, the lone big-screen holdout to date has been Jerry Seinfeld himself. Back in May 1995, *Variety*'s Michael Fleming reported that it might be some time before the public got a chance to rush to the multiplexes to watch Seinfeld work his *menschy* magic on the big screen: "Seinfeld has been much courted for feature work, but sources said he is apparently re-examining the downside of giving up a dream job—playing himself—for the murkier prospects of pix."

And lest we forget, the cast was being *paid* for their day job. But the question that kept more than a few *Seinfeld* fans up nights with added anxiety was: How long would they keep doing that job? Over the years, Seinfeld has been outspoken in predicting a relatively short run for the show. Early on, Seinfeld said that five seasons of the series were enough for him. This would be one case in which he happily would not be true to his word. Each time it had to be decided whether to push on or pack it in, Seinfeld would fortunately choose the former. "Maybe one more year," he was quoted as saying by the *Daily News*'s Marilyn Beck and Stacy Jenel Smith in a 1994 column. "I just want to make sure I complete it the right way."

After the fine 1995–1996 season—which included such triumphs as "The Engagement," "The Soup Nazi," "The Rye" and the season-ending "The Invitations"—Seinfeld ran up against the fact that he was going to have to complete the show the right way without the invaluable vision thing of his longtime comedy companion. Larry David wanted out. This decision would represent the biggest threat to *Seinfeld* since that annoying early matter of both getting on and staying on the air. Speaking to *Rolling Stone* in 1994, Carol Leifer described David and Seinfeld as "the Lennon-McCartney of comedy," and the idea of such a key, irreplaceable member leaving the *Seinfeld* group was a daunting one.

At the same time, it was probably not an altogether surprising idea, since David had apparently never hidden his angst about running the show. As Jason Alexander told *Entertainment Weekly*'s Lisa Schwartzbaum in the February 2, 1996, issue, "For Jerry, it's fun. For Larry, it's blood and agony." Seinfeld himself has always gone out of his way to credit David as being at the least an equal partner—in 1993 he told *Playboy*, "There is no show without him. He has, more than me, created this enterprise." (This year David created the feature film *Sour Grapes*, a comedy starring Steven Weber of *Wings* fame.)

The 1996–1997 season proved conclusively that there was indeed a show without David, though even without his hands-on participation as a writer-producer, the show continued to show his profound influence. Without his presence, *Seinfeld* was, to be sure, a slightly different show. Jerry's familiar stand-up introduction—already scaled back from the original prominent usage throughout episodes—was once and for all banished from *Seinfeld*. Still, the show would flourish right out of the box with a number of memorable episodes like "The Foundation," "The Bizarro Jerry," "The Little Kicks" and, yes, "The Yada Yada."

By the end of the 1996–1997 season,

FROM SOUP TO NAZI

A Review with Counter Intelligence—To Go

With the possible exception of Campbell's man Andy Warhol, nobody has done more for the hip quotient of soup than the great Al Yeganeh, the man whose succulent soups and brisk bisque-side manner were the basis for *Seinfeld*'s Soup Nazi episode (though Yeganeh has apparently always disdained the "Soup Nazi" name). In the winter of 1997, his real-life storefront—Soup Kitchen International, at 255A West 55th Street (at Eighth Avenue)—simmered up a big bowl of culinary controversy when the famed *Zagat*'s restaurant guide gave the Soup Kitchen an extraordinary twenty-seven out of a possible thirty points in the food category, not too shabby for a tiny takeout joint, especially when Le Cirque, one of the city's hottest restaurants *du jour,* only scored twenty-five for food. The media had a field day with this one, though reportedly Yeganeh was characteristically grumpy about the unwanted publicity. He was grumpy too when the New York media establishment besieged him with questions when Jerry Seinfeld announced his retirement, though he had no shortage of comments about Seinfeld. "I was so happy to go on the air and defend myself against that clown [Jerry Seinfeld], who gets on my nerves and just abuses me and uses me," he told the *New York Post.*

Our own recent taste test suggests that Yeganeh's place truly is a sort of heaven for soup lovers. Perhaps that explains why on a winter afternoon otherwise sane soup nuts—largely female (Ladies Love Cool A!)—were willing to wait on line for almost an hour with about seventy-five others in order to sample Yeganeh's wares. During the long wait, which most accepted gracefully, one could occupy the time small-talking about *Seinfeld,* checking out a nearby sign for Kramer's Reality Tour (see "The Real Kramer: A Magical Mystery Tour with Snacks," page 47) or simply preparing for a close encounter with Al himself.

As it turns out, Yeganeh's behavior was businesslike, if somewhat grimly so, and he showed none of the divalike madness seen on *Seinfeld*. A determinedly private man who follows his own rules, Yeganeh continues to operate his restaurant out of an actual hole in the wall. The master chef and his three or four helpers do their magic in a tiny kitchen half the size of Jerry's living room, and customers line up at an outside counter. The daily soup selections are posted on a board near the register, and this day's auspicious offerings from the gods included: shrimp bisque, chicken and broccoli, split pea, corn and potato chowder, mushroom chili and Hungarian beef goulash. When you (finally) get to the counter, you make your choice—no hesitation here—pay the bill and move to the left as quickly as possible (a moment of life imitating *Seinfeld* art). At six to eight dollars for a small bowl of soup, you might think the prices are as overinflated as Manhattan apartment rents, but Al and his minions lovingly pack up a bag for their grateful customers that contains not only the liquid gold, but bread, fruit and chocolate.

The mushroom chili—which seemed to be flavored with, among other things, a strong shot of vinegar—was hot enough to have brought an extra bead of sweat to Georgie Boy's brow, though he surely would be reaching for another bowl of the tasty, if unusual, soup. The corn and potato chowder, too, was worthy of seconds, but the bisque, Al's specialty, truly lived up to its hype—it was so delicious it could even make Jerry forget, temporarily, that ultimately it's only cereal that belongs in a bowl.

"maybe one more year" had become something of a *Seinfeld* mantra—after all, there were many parties interested in keeping the show going. There was a network that wanted to ensure that its Must-See TV gravy train stayed safely on track. There was Castle Rock, to whom the show was not only a source of pride but a significant profit center. And of course there was the viewing public, show, "We had asked years ago to be part of the profit participation. Everyone had said no. . . . We asked for this salary, which is insane, to compensate for what we didn't get when we were locked out of that." Alexander pointed out that somebody was going to have to spend all that money, since *Seinfeld* is a show that generates a couple hundred million dollars of profit a season.

Time magazine's estimate about how much each of the cast members makes per word:

Seinfeld $1,703.58
Alexander $1,056.34
Louis-Dreyfus $1,863.35
Richards $1,333.33

who—foolishly—wanted to continue having a truly outstanding, timeless comedy to watch.

In May 1997, a sort of comedic Cuban Missile Crisis erupted, with Jason Alexander, Julia Louis-Dreyfus and Michael Richards demanding a remarkable $1 million an episode in order to continue on for the next season. The request—while historic for "supporting" players on a series—was not without its reasoning. As Jason Alexander would later explain to Matt Lauer during an appearance on the *Today*

In the end, the three *Seinfeld* holdouts may not have gotten what they wanted, but they sure got what they needed. By May 26, 1997, *Time* reported that Alexander, Louis-Dreyfus and Richards had dropped their demand from $1 million per episode and settled for a measly $600,000 an episode for the next season's twenty-two–show run, up from the $160,000 they had made for the previous season. The ever-helpful *Time* went on to estimate how much each of the cast members would now be making per word: Seinfeld $1,703.58, Alexander

SEINING OFF
ED KOCH on *Seinfeld*

Like Seinfeld *itself, former mayor Ed Koch has been dismissed by some as "too New York."*
As with the show, such nay-saying has never stopped him from crossing over outside the five boroughs.
Currently, he can be seen dispensing jurisprudence on the successful syndicated revival of
The People's Court. *In his most recent novel* Murder on Thirty-fourth Street, *he's a detective and*
still mayor of New York ("my fantasy," admits Hizzoner) who solves the murder of Santa Claus.
We asked Koch to render a judgment on Seinfeld.

I am a *Seinfeld* fan. I don't watch it every week—the fact is, I probably see more reruns than the originals—but I think it's the smartest, most insightful program on the air, just *brilliant*. The episode on masturbation was probably the funniest one I've ever seen.

That "too New York" criticism was made before I went on the air, and the producer said, "What about *Seinfeld*? What about *Rosie*?" Well, you can't be any more New York than those two programs. So I guess those were people who didn't really have a feel for the high intelligence of the nation. I happen to believe that people around this country are very smart and always have been. New York has its own style. When I became mayor I think I added to the affection for New York—I wanted to convey that New York was the capital of New York and that we should be proud of it.

Has *Seinfeld* helped turn around New York? Oh, *sure*, I think it's a very positive statement for turning around people who might have a misconception about New Yorkers. I think when they see *Seinfeld*, they see events that could have happened in their town. I think they identify with those people—they're vulnerable, they're funny, they're intelligent. I mean, they're like your sisters and your brothers, your cousins, aunts and uncles . . . only with a special brand of neuroticism.

$1,056.34, Louis-Dreyfus $1,863.35 and Richards $1,333.33.

As awe-inspiring as those terms might appear, the show was still in many senses a bargain. As NBC Entertainment president Warren Littlefield said in May 1997 when announcing his network's new lineup for the fall, "Praise the Lord! *Seinfeld*'s back." *Business Week* reported Seinfeld was getting $22 million as an actor, writer and producer.

Not everyone was saying "Praise the Lord," of course. In a *New York Times* Op-Ed piece Maureen Dowd criticized the show, which she called "ever more self-referential and self-regarding," as well as referring to the show's "surreally greedy" actors.

S E I N I N G   O F F
AARON SPELLING on *Seinfeld*

The legendary television and film producer—not to mention Tori's dad—
has had numerous smash TV shows including Melrose Place, *a show that Jerry secretly admires,*
as revealed by a lie detector test in "The Beard."

We have thirty-seven copies of that episode! We felt very much complimented. No, I wouldn't have to take a lie detector to say I'm a fan of *Seinfeld*. It's probably the only comedy I really like. Why do I like it? Well, it's not joke-joke, it's character-character. I saw Jerry Seinfeld in Las Vegas once and I've been a fan of his ever since. The show is really tremendous. I don't see *Seinfeld* copied as much as *Friends* is emulated. I think with *Seinfeld* you can't copy it because of those four people. I mean they're all *so* spectacular. As far as a favorite character, I'd have to say Jerry, of course, but that sounds corny. He's the glue that holds it all together. He's the quarterback—every show needs a quarterback. I just hope next time they do *Beverly Hills 90210*!

Most viewers were simply thankful to have the chance to delay a dreaded if inevitable bout with *Seinfeld* withdrawal, a fearsome eventuality made less threatening by the comforting thought that at least we'll always have reruns.

The sometimes bumpy 1997–1998 season suggests that the returning *Seinfeld* team is not just in it for the money. After all, people are also well compensated for far, *far* lesser shows.

Still, all that money talk seemed to stir up at least a little ill will and harsh feelings. Critics started squawking once again about the show slipping—an odd charge in the age of *Moesha* and *Dr. Quinn, Medicine Woman*. In October 1997, the *New York Post* conducted a poll on whether viewers were satisfied with the first four episodes—48 percent were, 52 percent felt there was room for improvement. Seinfeld himself made a point to call the paper and said he was "flattered" to be worthy of a poll.

The truth is that right from the ninth season's opening episode, "The Butter Shave," it was clear that *Seinfeld* remains anything but a safe, boring sellout. What other show would kick off a season with scenes that could potentially offend the old, the handicapped and even the cannibals—all of whom could be in Nielsen families? Clearly, any show that can still be pushing buttons and pushing the envelope all these years down the line is doing something right.

Speaking to *60 Minutes*' Steve Kroft in 1996, Seinfeld offered that he was the happiest he had ever been in his life. "I never thought I could do what I'm doing now," he explained. "I'm very proud of the fact that I believed in myself and I turned out to have something, because I really didn't know. And so the fact that I bet on myself and didn't lose is a pretty deep reward."

Seinfeld's reward is, in this case, truly the gain of anyone who has access to a TV. *Seinfeld* has made a number of people rich, but it has made countless more happy. This remains a remarkable achievement. In 1994 when Steve Pond of *TV Guide* asked him what he was proudest of about the show, Jerry Seinfeld answered that "we've been on the air for six seasons, and we've done a hundred episodes, and we still haven't become a TV show. . . . We're still just doing twenty-two minutes of . . . something."

The bad news that Jerry Seinfeld had turned down $5 million an episode and would cease production at the end of *Seinfeld*'s ninth season became public knowledge right after Christmas in 1997. One imagines millions of distraught, shaken fans of the show turning instead to Festivas, since the traditional Yuletide will have negative associations from now on. Instantly, the selfsame media, which had spent the fall of 1997 overhyping some decline of the show's quality, kicked off what

looked certain to be an extended period of *Seinfeld* mourning.

The end of *Seinfeld* as a series was treated like a national tragedy because, in a sense, it was, at least for the fine folks at NBC, as well as anyone else in need of a dependable weekly comedy fix. The network was said to have made $500 million in 1997, some 40 percent of it coming from *Seinfeld*. "*Seinfeld* Loss Imperils NBC's Prime-Time Clout" warned one *Wall Street Journal* headline. In a lead Op-Ed piece entitled "The *Seinfeld* Universe" the *New York Times* acknowledged, "Some episodes about such absurdist miscellany as the male brassiere, the Soup Nazi and the love life of John Cheever have become national conversational references. . . . The beauty of *Seinfeld* was that art and life were often indistinguishable."

Ironically, the person who seemed least tortured by the decision to stop was the funny guy who turned down the not-so-small fortune. "This was between me and the show," Seinfeld told *Time*'s Bruce Handy in a January 1998 cover story. Perhaps unsurprisingly, Seinfeld compared the decision to stop the show to knowing when it was time to get offstage when doing stand-up. "If I get off now I have a chance at a standing ovation."

Not for nothing, the ovation for *Seinfeld* should last well into the twenty-first century.

The queen of "Get
out!" and two of her
trusty courtiers.

GET OUT!

AN UNBELIEVABLE TRUE-OR-FALSE QUIZ

Some of the following statements are incredible but true *Seinfeld*-related facts. Others are total pieces of crap that come to you directly from the fevered, sleep-deprived imagination of the author. Your assignment, should you choose to accept it, is to attempt to distinguish between the two groups.

1. Presidential progeny Chelsea Clinton makes a cameo appearance as an icy patron in "The Non-Fat Yogurt."

2. Jason Alexander and *ER*'s George Clooney both appeared in a short-lived mid-eighties TV series titled *E/R*. Clooney played Ace, the nephew of the head nurse, while Alexander was hospital administrator Harold Stickley.

3. Jerry Seinfeld and famed Amy Fisher associate Joey Buttafuoco reportedly graduated from the very same high school in Massapequa.

4. According to the *Los Angeles Times*, Germany's Cable 1—which canceled *Seinfeld* after less than a year's run—has enjoyed great success with the much beloved Nazi-themed sit-com *Hogan's Heroes*.

5. In "The Fusilli Jerry," it is finally revealed that Newman's first name is actually Paul.

6. Citing "his remarkable work that has advanced mankind in a variety of totally insignificant ways," Jason Alexander was awarded a MacArthur Foundation "genius" grant on the basis of his performance in "The Marine Biologist."

7. Both Michael Richards and Jason Alexander are Virgos.

8. Jerry Seinfeld has claimed to *Play-boy* that in real life he truly is the master of his domain.

9. Kathie Lee Gifford has gone on public record to state that Jerry Seinfeld's mother is funnier than David Letterman's mother.

10. Julia Louis-Dreyfus and Richard Dreyfuss appeared together in a critically acclaimed Showtime documentary about the Dreyfus case.

11. Michael Richards could be seen—though, due to poor ratings, probably rarely *was* seen—as Rick the gardener in the cast of the short-lived syndicated 1987 comedy called *Marblehead Manor*.

12. Jason Alexander once shared an apartment with actress Holly Hunter of *Broadcast News* and *The Piano* fame.

13. In a nod to "The Soup Nazi," there have reportedly been plans for a chain of Soup Nutsy restaurants.

14. Jerry Seinfeld opened for Guns n' Roses, performing twenty minutes of slashing stand-up on the Middle Eastern leg of the *Appetite for Destruction* tour.

15. In 1984, Jason Alexander starred as Tevye in an otherwise entirely black production of *Fiddler on the Roof* that proved unsuccessful during a spottily attended national dinner theater tour.

16. Mendys—featured prominently in "The Soup"—is actually a popular restaurant on Manhattan's Upper West Side.

17. Jason Alexander is the great-grandson of baseball great Grover Cleveland Alexander.

18. Julia Louis-Dreyfus won the 1995–1996 Emmy for Supporting Actress in a Comedy Series.

19. The United States Postmaster General has announced that a commemorative Newman stamp will be available to the general public in late 1998.

20. Jerry Seinfeld told *Rolling Stone* that his father used to play poker with famed organized-crime figure Carlo Gambino.

21. Noted character actor Art Vandalay came out of retirement to play the rabbi with loose lips in "The Postponement."

22. According to a 1997 report in the *Washington Post*, Vice President Al Gore is suspected of having made a series of fund-raising conference calls from the White House to the entire cast of *Seinfeld*.

23. According to a 1997 column by Marilyn Beck and Stacy Jenel Smith, Jerry Seinfeld rents an airplane hangar to house his considerable collection of Porsches.

THE REAL KRAMER
A Magical Mystery Tour with Snacks

Once upon a time in the Times Square area, Kenny Kramer lived across the hall from Larry David in Manhattan Plaza, an apartment development for performing artists meant to help clean up the Hell's Kitchen area. David has admitted to borrowing elements from Kenny Kramer for Cosmo Kramer, such as his stunning lack of any visible means of support.

Kenny Kramer is, fittingly enough, a real character. A former stand-up comic, band manager and jingle producer, who is now in his fifties, Kramer runs Kramer's Reality Tour, an amusing sight-seeing jaunt to assorted Manhattan landmarks that figure, however tangentially, in the *Seinfeld* series, complete with inside information, semi-spontaneous wit and, yes, snacks. All this and a few finely wasted hours for only $37.50.

Like any true *Seinfeld*-head in good standing, I had to check it out. Our journey began at an area theater close by Kramer's once and present Manhattan Plaza apartment. Kramer's cohost for this humorous happening was Bobby Allen Brooks, a vaguely Newmanesque comedy veteran who explained that Kramer was *his* best friend, even though he was in fact not Kramer's best friend. Kramer himself had some of the loony charm, wit and look of his namesake, with an even healthier appetite for self-promotion.

A Swingin' Time: Kramer apparently not at all teed off with the Reality Tour.

After a brief multimedia introduction at the theater—highlighted by a chance to see some rare Larry David stand-up footage—we hit the road. And while Mayor Rudy Giuliani may be overstating it a bit when he hyped the tour as "a valuable cultural and entertainment venture," it was a worthwhile journey through the heart of *Seinfeld* country. On his home page, Kramer himself bills the event as "a romp through what's factual and fantasy in the world of *Seinfeld*."

This author had a great deal of fun in an obsessive-compulsive kinda way, but sadly had to bail out midway at Tom's Diner on 112th Street and Broadway—seen in the Monk's Cafe establishing shot—in order to attend his sister's wedding, though it was a tough call. By choosing family commitments over *Seinfeld* sites, I missed the Kramer-promised pizza and so the tour's cuisine cannot be reviewed here. Hey, even a *Seinfeld* freak must make certain sacrifices.

Sadly, Kenny Kramer decided to stop personally running the tour, though it no doubt remains a total trip. For further information and reservations, call 1-800-KRAMERS or, from outside these United States, 212-268-5525. By all means, jump aboard this magic bus.

Cereal killers Elaine and Jerry bond over a beloved breakfast food.

24. Due to the protests of a small but vocal anti-Semitic political faction centered near Cannes, *Seinfeld* has never been broadcast anywhere in France.

25. Jerry Seinfeld served as host for an NBC special entitled *Spy TV: How to Become Famous* associated with the humor magazine *Spy*.

26. Jerry Seinfeld has made only ten appearances on *The Tonight Show* with Jay Leno and *The Late Show* with David Letterman.

27. Jason Alexander appeared in a TV movie called *Senior Trip* with master thespian and former *Joanie Loves Chachi* icon Scott Baio.

28. Elaine won "The Contest."

29. In 1995 Jason Alexander told the graduating class of Boston University's School for the Arts in a commencement address, "Fame, this thing I have, is very rare, very strange, very meaningless."

30. Jason Alexander once appeared in a TV movie called *Sexual Healing*

along with Anthony Edwards and Helen Hunt.

31. Michael Richards can be spotted briefly as a narcoleptic death rock roadie from Cleveland in the famed rock satire *Spinal Tap*.

32. Though a long-standing ratings success, *Seinfeld* remarkably has never actually appeared at the very top of the weekly Nielsen ratings—its best-ever ranking was number 2.

33. According to the July 1, 1997, edition of the *National Enquirer*, "Jerry Seinfeld became obsessed with a big-breasted flight attendant and refused to let anyone else serve him on the plane."

34. Jerry Stiller was in the cast of *Tattingers*, a TV series about a Manhattan restaurant—later reworked as *Nick & Hillary*—which also featured Blythe Danner, Stephen Collins, Rob Morrow and Chris Elliott.

35. Jason Alexander reportedly proposed to his wife on a Times Square billboard.

36. Seinfeld has said that the name of his Long Island hometown, Massapequa, means "by the mall" in Indian.

37. In the late eighties, Julia Louis-Dreyfus toured the Far East in *Lady Bird Sings the Blues*, a David Mamet–penned one-woman show concerning the trying life and times of Lady Bird Johnson.

38. Jason Alexander has discussed plans to star in a musical version of the classic Ernest Borgnine film *Marty* on Broadway.

39. Jerry Seinfeld has been quoted as saying that a George spin-off would have to be titled *This Poor Man*.

40. The angst-ridden band Nirvana made a brief guest appearance as the band that moves into Jerry's apartment building in the 1991 episode "The Apartment."

41. In June of 1994, Jerry Seinfeld was presented with an honorary doctorate by Queens College, his alma mater.

42. In the months before her tragic death, the late Princess Diana was in serious negotiations to play a Cockney love interest for Kramer in a very special one-hour episode of *Seinfeld*.

43. Jerry Seinfeld ate cereal during his first meeting with Julia Louis-Dreyfus.

44. In 1993, Larry David served as executive producer on a short-lived TV series based on Mel Brooks's film *Life Stinks*.

SEINING OFF
JEFF FOXWORTHY on *Seinfeld*

Foxworthy is the former IBM computer engineer from Georgia who quit his job fifteen years ago and became a stand-up phenomenon, with best-selling albums and books. His own sitcom ran on both ABC and NBC, albeit briefly. And though the southern-fried comedian might seem a country cousin to Seinfeld, *Foxworthy definitely relates to his funny Yankee brethren.*

I've been told before that I was "too New York" and "too Jewish" too, so I can sympathize with Jerry. (*Laughs.*) Listen, I've had conversations with Jerry about this and the truth is, funny is funny. Trust me, I have friends in Georgia who have never left the state, have never been to New York City, and they watch *Seinfeld* religiously because it's funny. I've always been an admirer of Jerry.

I'm very impressed with how he was able to create the perfect TV vehicle for himself. I wasn't able to do it—it's a very, very difficult thing to do. I had talked to Jerry about it—I actually asked Jerry about this: "How do you do this? How do you get them to trust you to do it the way you want to?" And I think he had some of those frustrations early on. I think the fact that Jerry had Larry was key, and that Larry had such a clear vision of what Jerry's show should be. So it was like two people with a vision instead of one. I saw Larry perform in New York and I always loved his writing, but Larry didn't ever seem to enjoy performing that much. I would say to Jerry, "I'm trying to do a show and I've got four hundred people telling me how it should be." But he made it work, and I think he had to work on that a little bit in the beginning, but God, he did it great.

What I love about *Seinfeld* was that he was able to capture the essence of his stand-up and put it in a sitcom format. When I write, I know I'm always looking for those things that are common and universal. And with Jerry—even before the show—his comedy was almost always about taking the littlest, least funny thing he could find, and making it funny. He's a genius at that. For instance, standing in line at the post office. My first reaction as a comic is there's nothing funny about that. And he made it hilarious. And he was able to do that with the show. Now you have so many TV executives claiming they're partially responsible for *Seinfeld,* and guess what—they're *not.* They wouldn't have ever believed it would have worked. The only reason they picked the show up at all was so they would have an option left on Jerry.

For a favorite episode, it's hard to beat "master of your domain." Having done a TV show, I know the red flags that go up any time you mention anything out of the norm, much less to be able to do a show about *masturbation.* Only Jerry and Larry are smart enough to pull it off. *[Author's note: Interesting turn of phrase.]*

On our show, we worked right around the corner from *Seinfeld,* and around midnight at the Christmas party one of our cast members—who shall remain nameless because he probably wants to work again in television—swiped Jerry's golf cart, the one that takes Jerry all around the lot. We decided to turn it into a redneck golf cart, so we put that fringe around the top, put a Dolly Parton poster and big Christmas tree air fresheners in it, Super-Glued a compass to the front, put in leopard-skin seat covers—we really converted it, then took it back and left it for Jerry. And we thought we were going to battle, and we braced ourselves and then . . . nothing ever happened. I ran into Jerry one day, and said, "Man, you never did *anything*." And Jerry said, "We kept talking about it, but then we got so busy working on the show, we never came up with anything." Then I got to thinking—wait a minute, Jerry's coming in number one every week and I'm coming in number seventy . . . maybe *that's* why.

45. To make money in his pre-stardom days, Jerry Seinfeld once sold lightbulbs over the telephone.

46. Wayne Knight won a bronze medal for shot-putting at the 1984 Summer Olympics.

47. Phil Bruns, who originally played Jerry's dad, was also in the cast of *The Jackie Gleason Show* from 1964 to 1966.

48. Michael Richards has appeared as Kramer on an episode of *Mad About You.*

49. At the 1997 Jerry Lewis Labor Day Muscular Dystrophy Telethon, Jerry Seinfeld turned up and told Jerry Lewis, "You are one of my greatest idols. I always thought, 'There's a person named Jerry, and he's successful. Maybe I could do it.'"

50. At one point Kramer was going to be called Hoffman.

51. Jerry Seinfeld has entirely abandoned doing stand-up ever since the pilot episode of *Seinfeld* appeared.

52. Michael Richards thanked Dr. Robert Stein, a Jungian analyst he'd worked with, during one of his Emmy acceptance speeches.

53. Early in his stand-up days, Seinfeld was told by comic Jackie Mason, "It makes me sick, you're going to be such a big hit."

54. Jerry Seinfeld brought his mother, Betty, to the 1993 Emmys.

55. Jason Alexander appeared in a Los Angeles production of *Promises, Promises* along with Barney Martin, who plays Jerry's father on *Seinfeld.*

56. The four *Seinfeld* stars spent a night together in the Lincoln Bedroom—in one king-size bed.

Holy *Shtick*: George takes a comic leap of faith in "The Conversion."

FUNNY, YOU DON'T LOOK *SEINFELD*-ISH

A TRUE ZEALOT'S READING OF *SEINFELD* SCRIPTS AS HOLY *SHTICK*-TURE

Some spiritual searchers will look to the New Testament for the answers to life's more vexing moral issues, some to the slightly-older-but-still-in-fine-condition Old Testament. Some will quote the Koran, and still others look to Scientology and the writings of L. Ron Hubbard for the pause that refreshes. Personally, in moments of doubt and crisis, I look not to the cookie—as Jerry suggests in "The Dinner Party"—but rather to *Seinfeld* in order to regain both my spiritual and comical center.

In the final reckoning, scholars will have their own interpretations of the lessons of *Seinfeld*, providing a great testament to the depth of the wisdom found in the spirited yet humorous text. That said, there will be strict fundamen-

talists and others who foolishly see *Seinfeld* as simply "a TV show." But how could anything be as good as *Seinfeld* unless He—and I ain't talking about Warren Littlefield here, baby—wanted it to be thus? Forgive them, Jerry Seinfeld and Larry David, for the remaining few *Seinfeld* nonbelievers know not what they say. *Seinfeld*-ism has much to teach all who are willing to hear its timeless message of self-serving hope. Sometimes these lessons are elusive; there are in truth few commandments in the world of *Seinfeld* other than this golden rule: "Thou shalt not bore."

Must we really love our neighbor?

Well, if thy neighbor happens to be Kramer, the answer apparently is yes, we must. But it seems clear from Jerry's behavior in "The Kiss Hello" episode—in which the people in his building get overly friendly—that there are limits to how much we have to love our neighbors, especially if they're needy pains in the ass.

Is monogamy truly the way to go?

Earlier religions have offered varied views. *Seinfeld*-ism—taken as a collective whole—seems to suggest that we should be monogamous with a different preferably attractive character each and every week. Thus we can clearly deduce the loving God of *Seinfeld*—our good Lord of laughter—is an extremely loving and reasonable and even horny one.

So is God dead?

No, and George's sexually motivated religious quest in "The Conversion" at least shows him searching for some answers, albeit for the most shallow of reasons imaginable. My very best guess here is that God is not dead, but Susan quite clearly is.

Is man ultimately good?

Well, he can be okay—*Seinfeld* has demonstrated that we can for a time love the Drake or Keith Hernandez, for instance. Then, on the other hand, we must consider the existence of Newman, Bania and Crazy Joe Davola. So, in short, probably not.

Is there really such a place as heaven?

This remains unclear at this point, but there is some amazing soup right here on earth. And there's always Monk's, which has a pretty heavenly big salad.

So what exactly is the meaning of life?

Arguably, life as seen on *Seinfeld* is about a whole lot of nothing. It's about filling the time until we go the way of Susan and Nana. Less cynically, it's about comfort food and the bankrupt company of friends.

What happens to us when we die?

Well, in the case of Susan Biddle Ross, you get a goofy do-good foundation created in your name. You can also expect precious little mourning from your intended. Generally speaking, however, this issue has not been covered in any significant way, though there have been intimations that it could be addressed in the show's final episode. Death means at the very least the tragic loss of roomy, rent-controlled apartments.

Does God love Seinfeld?

Again, though there is little to no actual scriptural support for this position, I personally take it as a matter of faith that God loves *Seinfeld* as much as the next earthly viewer. Hey, look at the ratings—they're out of this world.

Must we actually honor our mother and father?

If by honor you mean must we make pilgrimages down to Florida retirement communities to see the old-timers, then the text makes it clear that the answer is yes. If you mean must we wish we could live forever in Queens with the crusty Costanzas, then the answer is a big no.

Finally, in terms of the existence of evil, why the hell was that lousy serpent brought into the Garden?

Based on the existence of Newman, we can only assume that the serpent was put here on earth to deliver the mail.

THE FOOLS

Network-Tested Secrets to Seeking Out Highly Dysfunctional Relationships on a Weekly Basis as Seen in Seinfeld

Bookstores are already filled with a wide variety of literature to help you figure out how to snare a spouse. But what about the poor individual looking for a different kind of resource, something that will help her or him find a *bad* relationship with absolutely no future? In addition to being so damned entertaining, *Seinfeld* is just such a resource, educating us on how to successfully avoid meaningful relationships well into early middle age and perhaps even beyond.

While *Seinfeld* is not written by professional therapists, one gets the distinct feeling that this Upper West Side–set show is written by people who have, shall we say, a certain extreme comfort level and familiarity with the need for a little healthy couch time.

For those poorly adjusted relationship-phobes bent on keeping their screwed-up solo status, *Seinfeld* is overripe with information to be gleaned about strategies on how to avoid becoming committed as long as humanly possible, as well as how to find the least appropriate, most toxic partner possible.

As Julia Louis-Dreyfus told *Playboy*'s David Rensin in 1996, "Many sexual topics, including masturbation, are broached humorously on this show, and they haven't been elsewhere on television. But let's not kid ourselves—a TV show isn't going to make a difference when it comes to communication between the sexes." But maybe—just maybe—we can indeed learn a great deal about what *not* to do by watching *Seinfeld* closely. What follows are some of the rules of romantic engagement as seen through the looking-glass of a show in which engagements have a funny way of ending in death—fifty ways to leave your lover, or to get your lover to leave you.

Fool #1: Try to Confine All of Your Meaningful Adult Romantic Relationships to No More Than Thirty Minutes

If relationships are war—and face it, boys and girls, they *are*—then at least attempt to make all your romantic entanglements limited, winnable wars—kind of like Vietnam, only with a happier ending. This fool also helps allow for the maximum number of attractive new guest stars in the sack per season.

Fool #2: Be Judgmental. Be *Very* Judgmental

Seinfeld's master of excuses in ending relationships is, of course, Jerry. With very few exceptions like, say, Keith Hernandez, Jerry is monumentally aloof and diligent in his fault-finding. His excuses actually lead to some other bizarro sub-fools such as Don't Be Dumped by Newman, Don't Even Consider Sharing a Toothbrush, Don't Wear Just One Outfit and Don't Confess to Liking Dockers Ads. All this went out the window for one fall 1997 episode, "The Serenity Now," in which Jerry gets briefly emotional and even proposes to Elaine. Hey, any fool can have an off day of commitment.

Fool #3: Bring Along a Chaperon

You'll never conquer Miss Rhode Island and make her a Mrs. when you have a squeaky third wheel like Kramer along for the ride.

Fool #4: Just Play at Being Married

See "The Wife," in which a bit of pre-marital play-acting ruins Jerry's relationship with no less a Must-See babe than Courteney Cox.

Fool #5: Spend an Obsessive Amount of Time with Your Friends to the Exclusion of All Others

Conveniently, there appears to be no single table at Monk's Cafe big enough to accommodate the *Seinfeld* gang and their significant others, should they decide to keep them on for more than a week at a time.

Fool #6: Make Your Masturbation Habits a Matter of Public Record

A self-serving way—as evidenced in "The Contest"—to remain the master of your own lonely domain forever.

Fool #7: Sleep with Old Flames Who've Since Become Your Closest Friends

What better way to ensure that you will eventually break up with somebody you've slept with than to sleep with someone with whom you've already broken up? See Jerry and Elaine's last tango in Manhattan in "The Deal."

Fool #8: Become More Attracted to People Simply Because Your Friends Find Them Attractive

See Jerry's reaction to Kramer's reaction to his love *thang* in "The Soul Mate."

Fool #9: Become Instantly Attracted to Your Best Friends' Exes as Soon as They Split Up

A related fool to #8. See Jerry's strange attraction to George's strange southern belle in "The Ex-Girlfriend."

Fool #10: Never Allow Your New Significant Other to Fully Bond with Your Own Cast of Buddies

This kind of interaction will only make love interests want to have a recurring role in your life, and that can get very expensive. See George's freak-out over Elaine's nascent bonding with Susan in "The Pool Guy."

Fool #11: Feel Free to Say "I Love You" Way Too Early in a Relationship

See George's faux pas in "The Face Painter."

Fool #12: By All Means, Go Right Ahead and Have Indiscriminate Sex in the Workplace

See George's job- and relationship-ending desk tryst in "The Red Dot" as well as his being driven to distraction in "The Secretary."

Fool #13: Put Your Buddies in a Seaside Context Where They Can All See Your Date Nude Before You Do

This is the ugly naked truth experienced by George in "The Hamptons."

Fool #14: Be Insensitive to Any Contemporary Notions of Political Correctness in Your Gift Giving

See how Jerry is able to undermine any possibility of lifelong happiness with a Native American woman simply by buying an offensive piece of statuary in "The Cigar Store Indian."

Fool #15: Look to Your Parents as Role Models for What Not to Do—Get Married

Spending even a few stolen moments with the Costanzas—or to a lesser extent with the Seinfelds or Mr. Benes—can be enough to put anyone off family life and keep even the partially romantic fully committed to the single life.

Fool #16: Convert to Another Religious Faith on a Whim

As George does in "The Conversion," change faiths for that highest and holiest of purposes—to keep scoring with a babe of another religion.

Fool #17: Pick Your Nose

This pick and move is sure to turn off the supermodel in your life, as it does for Jerry in "The Pick."

Fool #18: Why Not Feature Your Nipple on a Seasonal Card of Good Cheer?

This turns out to be more effective than mistletoe in getting the wrong kind of interest for Elaine in "The Pick."

Fool #19: Accidentally Lead the Media to Believe You're Otherwise Engaged with the Same Sex—Not That There's Anything Wrong with That

Watch Jerry and George meet the press in "The Outing" for the most effective way to extinguish interest from that annoying opposite sex.

Fool #20: Fake Orgasms and Then Years Later Tell Your Partner

I'll have one of what Elaine's not having in "The Mango."

Fool #21: Base Relationships on Things That Really Matter . . . Like Punctuation Usage

See "The Sniffing Accountant," which proves that Elaine—as befits any dedicated publishing type—values language enough to make relationship decisions based on an absence of exclamation points.

Fool #22: Pursue Virgins Who Will Only Give It Up for a Man with a Direct Tie to Camelot

In "The Virgin" we learn that some women are destined only to end up sharing their sexual inauguration with a Kennedy.

Fool #23: Share Your Special Unbeatable Bedtime "Move" with Others

As we see so painfully in "The Fusilli Jerry," it's dangerous to share your best tricks of the trade with every Tom, Dick or Dave Puddy.

Fool #24: Dance *Really, Really* Badly

If you dare, see Elaine getting down and funky in "The Little Kicks" and see how a bad case of dance fever can help you lose friends and influence people to run in the opposite direction.

Fool #25: Date Someone Who Is Almost Exactly Like You

Everybody knows that opposites attract, so why not go the other way like Jerry, who meets his near exact match with Jeannie Steinman (played by Janeane Garofalo) in "The Invitations."

Fool #26: Go Out with People Who Won't Admit That You're Dating Them

Ladies, this is the ultimate in men who can't commit, as evidenced by Elaine and Todd Gack who spend time together in "The Calzone." Similarly, as seen in "The Secret Code," the fact that someone can't even remember who you are can make them very appealing.

Fool #27: Forget About Dating Available Women When You Can Become Obsessed with an Oscar-Winning Actress

This fool works especially well when you happen to be engaged, as Georgie Boy is when he finds himself hung up on Marisa Tomei in "The Cadillac."

Fool #28: Get a Vanity License Plate That Really Communicates Your Inner Soul—Like "Assman"

Be like Kramer, who accidentally makes himself the butt of jokes in "The Fusilli Jerry."

Fool #29: The Job Makes the Man, So Try and Show Absolutely No Visible Means of Support

Come to think about it, this doesn't seem to have hurt Kramer much either.

Fool #30: Try to Date Hit-and-Run Drivers

What better way to make sure your special someone is irresponsible, as Jerry shows us in "The Good Samaritan."

Fool #31: Be Attracted to Neo-Nazis

As we see in "The Limo," all Nazis aren't bad looking, so why not flirt with fascists?

Fool #32: Screw Professional Ethics, Go Ahead and Travel the Globe with Your Creepy Therapist

If therapy works so well on a couch, then perhaps it can work even better in bed, as Elaine explores during a crazy European vacation with the not-so-good Dr. Reston in "The Pitch/The Ticket."

Fool #33: Go Ahead, Ladies, Date a Musician

Better yet, make it a slick saxophonist with sexual hang-ups, as Elaine does in "The Rye."

Fool #34: Don't Share Important Things—Like Your Bank Card Secret Code—with Your Loved One

This was just one more example of what was so wrong—and thus for our purposes here so right—with the pairing of George and the late Susan, truly a couple for our times.

Fool #35: Date Really Annoying Brits

Elaine remains the queen of meeting moronic men from the motherland, like the moocher who once stayed at her pad in "The Soup" and the double-crossing British clerk she dates in "The Wig Master."

Fool #36: Date People Who Steal Dialogue from the Collected Works of Neil Simon

Jerry does this in "The Plagiarizer," and really, is there a better way to stay a lifelong heartbreak kid?

Fool #37: Have Your Pal Burn Down the Cabin of Your Girlfriend's Parents

See talking head Kramer burning down the house in "The Bubble Boy."

Fool #38: Feel Free to Date Psychos/ Potential Stalkers Who Have the Word *Crazy* in Their Name

There's a certain truth in advertising with characters like Crazy Joe Davola, whom Elaine gets to know in "The Watch" and who reacts badly to a breakup in "The Opera."

Fool #39: Get Close to a Close-Talking Man

Paradoxically, this can be a good way to keep one's distance in the long term, as Elaine found with Aaron in "The Raincoats."

Fool #40: While You're At It, Why Not Find Yourself a Low-Talking Gal?

That's what Kramer did in "The Puffy Shirt," and soon enough he didn't have to hear her voice at all.

Fool #41: Sleep Late and Cause Your Significant Other to Miss Important Events

Elaine has shown the ability to sleep her way right out of a relationship, as she does with wake-up service worker James in "The Wink."

Fool #42: Be Allergic to His Pets

This is the other compelling reason the petting must end for Elaine in "The Wink."

Fool #43: When All Else Fails, Make Sure to Buy Really Cheap Wedding Invitations with Toxic Glue

This effective strategy should be self-explanatory. OK, she died, but at least it got George out of a close call with maturity.

Fool #44: Date a Woman Doing Hard Time in the Hopes That Our Penal System Will Keep Her Safely Behind Bars and Thus Out of Your Hair

There is one problem with behind-bars babes—occasionally they can bust out, as Celia does to George's distress in "The Little Jerry."

Fool #45: Rather Than Finding Available Singles, Make Sport of and Take a Shot at Splitting Up an Established Couple

That's what Jerry and Elaine conspire to do to Beth and David in "The Wait Out" and it works out fine, if frustratingly, for them all. After all, they end up flying solo once again, the ideal in the *Seinfeld* world.

Fool #46: Date the Kind of Confident, Forward Men Who Will Take "It" Out on a Date

This hands-on approach worked for Elaine in "The Stand In."

Fool #47: When Your Boyfriend Falls Seriously Ill, Don't Panic. Take the Time to Regain Your Composure and Buy Some Candy

This is an especially good idea if the candy in question happens to be Jujyfruits, as in "The Opposite."

Fool #48: Date Women with Laughs That Scare You

As Jerry finds out, grating characteristics—like a frightening laugh—can turn out to be positive. They allow one to move on to next week's love interest.

Fool #49: Date Your Buddy's Doppelgängers

A familiar gender-bending mistake—also known as the Mick and Bianca Jagger syndrome—that George makes, much to his heterosexual chagrin in "The Cartoon," during which some observers note a curious resemblance between Jerry and Ricky Nelson's lovely little girl.

Fool #50: Make Up to Break Up

Take a page from the Elaine handbook and Stylistics songbook, and return again and again to the scenes of your past romantic crimes, as Elaine did in the ninth season when she forgot about the failings of her face-painting boy toy, Puddy, and kept giving him one more chance.

UPCOMING TITLES FROM YOUR FRIENDS AT PENDANT PUBLISHING

Following in the footsteps of the overwhelmingly successful *The Fools: Network-Tested Secrets to Seeking Out Highly Dysfunctional Relationships on a Weekly Basis as Seen in Seinfeld* (over one hundred copies sold, editions published in fifteen countries including Israel and New Jersey), Pendant Publishing is proud to present a new line of books focused on the cast of *Seinfeld: Seinfeld on the Couch: Popular Shrinkage*, a series of titles by David Wild, Mh.D. (Master of His Domain).

Books in the *Seinfeld on the Couch: Popular Shrinkage* series will offer gang analysis and case histories of Jerry Seinfeld, George Costanza, Elaine Benes, Cosmo Kramer and the men and women who love them.

For nine seasons now, *Seinfeld* has made dysfunction the new American pastime. Why not cut back on those costly therapy bills by turning instead for all your head-shrinking needs to these "scholarly" tomes that put *Seinfeld* on the couch where it so obviously belongs?

SEINFELD *FRIENDSHIP: BOND OR BONDAGE?*

Are Jerry, George, Elaine and Cosmo just hanging around, or are they in fact profoundly hung up? Wild takes a long, hard, analytic look at the tortured "I'm Not Okay, You're Even Less Okay" relationships that for better and worse are at the very poisoned heart of *Seinfeld*.

SOUP NAZIS, BIG SALADS AND OTHER FOOD ISSUES: SEINFELD *'S HEARTY APPETITE FOR DISASTER*

When the gang goes to Monk's Cafe, what are they *really* hungry for? Always a biting social critic, Wild snacks on the *Seinfeld* gang's all-you-can-eat buffet load of personal problems, from Jerry's clearly infantile cereal fixation to Elaine's need for the big salad. You'll chew on some big questions, such as: Why exactly can't these people simply accept the fact that non-fat yogurt has no fat? Finally, a healthy way to digest the question that's bigger than the Big Salad: What's eating *these* people?

JERRY: STAND-UP GUY OR PETER PAN WITH A PUNCH LINE?

Wild dares to ask what happens when the laughter ends and at long last the growing up begins. How has Jerry nurtured and even coddled his inner child into early middle age? Is everything a joke to this guy? Who *is* this person? A sober perspective on a funnyman who's never put away childish things, like his cereal, Superman and, well, Georgie Boy.

THE COSMETOLOGY OF KRAMER: MEN ARE FROM MARS, COSMO IS FROM . . . ?

You'll want to file this brutally frank Freudian investigation under "Advanced Abnormal Psych." Examining Kramer

A Sane Man in an Insane World: Criminally cool Kramer looking splendid in his Amazing Technicolor Dreamcoat.

from his hazy beginnings with Babs to his "adult" life as the walking id with the big hair, Wild seeks to examine central issues: Could it be that Kramer makes such a big deal of his entrances because he's a man-child who's got a big problem with good-byes? Or as Wild asks alternatively, is Kramer really just a sane man in an insane world?

ELAINE BENES: TOMBOY OR TIME BOMB WAITING TO GO OFF?

You'll want to rush out and purchase this gem of a gender issue study, which puts Elaine on a comfy couch and grills her like the not-so-good Dr. Reston does about why *Seinfeld*'s riot grrrl with a certain *Camelot*-like grace ends up spending so much time acting like one of the boys. A postfeminist point of view guides us through the strange turns taken by *Seinfeld*'s curviest character.

GEORGE COSTANZA: ANGST IN HIS SWEATPANTS

George gets buck naked—psychologically speaking only—in this intimate study of the balding man who could only say "I love you" to a dog. A look at a selfish, petty but lovable man who wears insecurity and dishonesty like a too-tight pair of chinos. Wild looks deep into the Costanza family tree in order to get a front-row seat to the making of a mess.

WASH & WEARY: THE DIRTY, MESSY TRUTH ABOUT JERRY'S CLEANLINESS

An extremely neat little treatise concerning Jerry's obsessive-compulsive disorder, *Wash & Weary* attempts to tidy up all previous theoretical inquiries about Seinfeld's need for control and his tendency to break off relationships for the smallest infraction of personal grooming. For Jerry, cleanliness may not be next to godliness, but rather madness.

NEWMAN'S OWN: BIG MAN, BIGGER PROBLEMS

In *Newman's Own*, Wild tackles perhaps his biggest and weightiest subject yet. A postal pathology of the man who inherited the Son of Sam's mail route. For Wild, Newman isn't really mad at Jerry—no, Newman's real worst enemy is, of course, *Newman*. Wild offers a stirring explanation for some of Newman's less appetizing characteristics—a grand variation on the Twinkie Defense that takes into account a far wider range of junk foods.

CRAZY JOE DAVOLA AND THE INSANITY DEFENSE

Who is Crazy Joe Davola and why is everybody saying all these terrible things about him? And ultimately just how crazy is Crazy Joe Davola anyway? Wild suggests it may be more accurate, com-

Desktop Publisher: Elaine ponders another best-selling title for the Pendant Publishing catalog.

passionate and productive to refer to him publicly as Misunderstood Joe Davola, Sanity-Challenged Joe Davola or possibly Improperly Reared and Toilet-Trained Joe Davola.

THE SEINFELDS AND THE COSTANZAS: TWO APPROACHES TO PARENTHOOD FROM POTTY TRAINING ON

A comparative look at the approaches to child rearing as they were practiced by the Seinfelds and the Costanzas with a parentally supportive eye to figuring out why these people have sustained adolescence into early middle age. Also, a look at the deep-seated reasons the two sets of parents have a tendency to feud like the Capulets and the Montagues with New York accents.

"THE PANTIES YOUR MOTHER LAID OUT FOR YOU": SEXUAL PERVERSITIES IN MANHATTAN

For strict Freudians, *Seinfeld* has always been less a show about nothing than a show about getting laid. Freud stressed the importance of work and love in a healthy adult life. Since work can be elusive in the world of *Seinfeld*, love—physical love—becomes important. A frank and explicitly adult look at a group of lovable perverts who have made a funny fetish of their own neuroses.

In addition, these other titles are expected by the end of the millennium:

> *Seinfeld of Dreams*
>
> *Elaine's Dancing: Movement or Madness?*
>
> *Zen and the Art of Seinfeld*
>
> *Elaine's "Get Out" Gesture as a Reflection of Postfeminist Rage*
>
> *Mr. Pitt: Publishing Patriarch as Father Figure*
>
> *Frank and Estelle Costanza: Can This Marriage Be Saved?*
>
> *Homoeroticism on the West Side: Jerry and George—A Love Story for Our Times?*

SEINING OFF
DR. JOYCE BROTHERS on *Seinfeld*

Famed $64,000 Question *winner, psychologist and columnist Dr. Joyce Brothers is the sort of authority who could provide a little professional celebrity shrinkage on the mental health of the* Seinfeld *gang.*

So, Doctor, what do you make of the bond between these characters on **Seinfeld***?*

I think the friendship is something that we've all wished that we had. We all wish we had those people who we can depend on. And they can depend on each other even though there are problems there. There's a warmth and a caring among the group. They have adventures together—very few of us have had such close friendships and adventures. There's always some impediment, of course, but we like to see people overcome those impediments. And there are activities that we all have in our lives but we haven't seen them on-screen. For example, they have the kinds of problems that in any other show would get people absolutely hopping mad—orgasm, faking orgasm, masturbation. There was the scene where George comes out of the toilet and falls on his face but hasn't pulled his pants up. But it's done with such taste in tasteless situations that you enjoy seeing them walking the line.

Do you think they've made dysfunction a high art?

Well, I'm not sure that there's that much dysfunction here. Yes, there is a guy who can't keep a job and there's a gal who is by any stretch of the imagination a little bit promiscuous and so on. But they function. This is a *functional* dysfunctional group. They function because as part of a whole it all works out.

Are they sort of family in that way?

Yes, they are so interrelated that when they were renegotiating for more money you could not conceive of the show without all of the characters.

So has the show ultimately had a healthy impact on the American public?

Yes. Because it doesn't deal with the far-out, it deals with everyday life. And you can find humor and love and fun and excitement in things that happen to us all the time.

Do you have a favorite episode?

The one where they bring the bread. *[Author's note: That would be "The Rye," good Doctor.]*

S W E A T P A N T S   C H I C
The Style, Such as It Is, of Seinfeld

Though *Seinfeld* has launched fewer haircuts than its Thursday night pal *Friends,* and arguably even fewer than *60 Minutes,* the gang has had its own low-key style impact, promoting the Puffy Shirt, exploring the strange, adventurous world of the J. Peterman catalog, reviving the executive trench coat and presenting the urban sombrero, among other notable contributions to not-so-haute couture. Never has a situation comedy come clothed in such a far-flung and often funky ensemble of truly bad sweaters, cool Salvation Army oddities and lived-in sweatpants. Among their numerous other accomplishments, the often casual *Seinfeld* power quartet proves that not everyone has to dress for success. For as no less a prose fashion plate than Jonathan Swift wrote in a 1720 letter to a young clergyman, "Proper words in proper places make the true definition of style."

Ellen Tien—who with Valerie Frankel coauthored *Prime-Time Style: The Ultimate TV Guide to Fashion Hits—and Misses* (Perigee)—offers high praise for the less than high fashions of *Seinfeld* and the subtle work of the show's costume designer, Charmaine Simmons. "They dress the characters on *Seinfeld* for

Puff Daddy: Jerry dressed for success on the *Today* show in his Adam Ant–like Puffy Shirt.

comic effect," says Tien. "*Seinfeld* was the only show of all the shows we wrote about where they were really dressing for the sake of the show's sensibility.

"Kramer has the classic vaudeville look—they actually shorten his pants, which is an old vaudeville trick to make him look sort of clownish and goofy. They put him in things that he can move in for those entrances. They want things that aren't going to trip him up. Nothing is nice and neat on him. It's vintage stuff and big bold patterns. They also have to be sure that whatever they get for him they can get in doubles and triples. He could spill something on himself or split a seam with all the pratfalls."

As it turns out, George's discomfort isn't entirely existential. "They purposely put George all in clothes that are about a size too small," says Tien. "The idea is to make him look even more repressed; he looks like he's having even more of a difficult time, like he's sweating. They want his shirts too tight around the neck, ties that are on too tight, waistbands that are straining and sort of doubled over. I

> "They purposely put George all in clothes that are about a size too small. The idea is to make him look even more repressed, like he's sweating. I would say that George gets the raw end of the deal in terms of clothing because they shop for him at Penney's and Sears."
>
> —*Ellen Tien, coauthor of* Prime-Time Style

would say that George sort of gets the raw end of the deal in terms of clothing 'cause they shop for him at Penney's and Sears. They want him to really look like the average guy."

Elaine gets points for realism in that she repeats her outfits more than the average TV female. As for her look, "They want her to look very feminine, since she's the only woman among men—they want that contrast," says Tien. "They mix new and vintage clothes. To keep the feel, they put her in very dark, New Yorky colors—neutrals, browns, blacks. And I think when she started working for J. Peterman they made her even more eclectic.

"Jerry is the straight man and they set him up and dress him as the straight man," says Tien. "When they did the stand-up opening, the big concern was that he not just blend right into the curtain so all you'd see was the head. But they keep him very conservative, very plain, sort of subtle loose stuff."

Finally, there's the show's most substantial slab of beefsteak: No matter what the hell they stuff him into, Newman somehow looks good!

SCREENFELD

A CRITICAL FILMOGRAPHY OF THE *SEINFELD* CAST

There can be no doubt that the stars of *Seinfeld* are firmly entrenched as the masters of the small screen. But what—you ask for rhetorical reasons—of their place on the big screen? Both before and during *Seinfeld*, the show's cast members—with the notable exception of the impressively cautious Jerry Seinfeld—have appeared in many feature films, from major works of cinematic art to major wipeouts of movie trash. In doing so, they have made the transition far better than most.

Sure, in our celluloid history there certainly have been many perfectly fine movies somehow made without a single *Seinfeld* cast member—that *Citizen Kane* flick was pretty watchable, for example. Still, who among us hasn't pondered how much better many films of the past could have been with at least a semblance of that *Seinfeld* right stuff? Imagine *Raging Kramer* or *Mr. Costanza's Opus*. And

wouldn't *Titanic* have been really big if it had a *Seinfeld* cast member in it? Of course, one could understand some nervous auteurs not wanting to overwhelm a film with a strong *Seinfeld* association—after all, for me the biggest and most fearsome creature in that *Jurassic Park* picture will always be Newman's own Wayne Knight, not all those silly dinosaurs. Similarly, for the true *Seinfeld* fanatic—the one who worships the show, as Ricky in "The Cigar Store Indian" does *TV Guide*—it was Knight too who flew to the greatest dramatic heights in *Space Jam.* (When I found my eye drawn to Knight rather than Nicole Kidman during their scenes together in Gus Van Sant's *To Die For,* I knew I was watching too much *Seinfeld.*)

The following section offers a retrospective of the full-length feature films, already released as this book goes to print, that feature one of the *Seinfeld*

Hair Apparent: George with Jerry and a very different, nonhooking pretty woman.

leads. The key word is *seen*, meaning that films with just the voice of a *Seinfeld* star—such as Alexander's voicings in *The Return of Jafar* (1994) and *The Hunchback of Notre Dame* (1996), in which he's the voice of Hugo, a chatty gargoyle—are not included. Don't worry, *Seinfeld* fans, there will be many more films to come from our *Seinfeld* thespians. I'm sure I'll see you at the movies and in the video stores, looking for a free copy of *Rochelle Rochelle*.

The Jason Alexander Oeuvre

THE BURNING
(1981 or 1980)
Director: Tony Maylam

As a piece of filmmaking, *The Burning* makes *Friday the 13th* look like *Psycho*. Still, this nickel-and-dime-budget slasher-at-a-summer-camp piece of crap is well worth searching out for a number of curious reasons. For example, make it through a half hour of horror hilarity at Camp Blackfoot and you can see an incredibly young and hairy Jason Alexander and Fisher Stevens flash a memorable moon by the camp's lakeside. Alexander plays Dave, a jockish and almost macho camper given to wearing a jersey with the number 96. One imagines George Costanza's summer vacations were never like this. Alexander's hardly alone in this bloody mess: In addition to Stevens as a long-haired camper named Woodstock, there's Holly Hunter, a friend and one-time apartment mate of Alexander's who makes her screen debut as a camper named Sophie. Amazingly, Miramax's Harvey Weinstein had a hand in penning this pandering piece of piffle, which offers death and T & A in equal measure. But on the other hand, how many chances do you get to see the actor who inhabits George so believably canoeing on film?

THE MOSQUITO COAST
(1986)
Director: Peter Weir

A powerful, somewhat underappreciated adaptation of Paul Theroux's novel, with a fine cast including Harrison Ford, River Phoenix and Helen Mirren, *The Mosquito Coast* made some waves by casting screen idol Ford in a surprisingly unsympathetic role. Little noted at the time was the much bigger and less remarked upon stretch of Jason Alexander, who popped up very early in the proceedings as a seemingly unhappy hardware store worker who takes a little abuse from difficult customer Ford. The credits list Alexander's role as "Clerk"—though I would argue that he deserved a substantially larger credit like, say, "Pissed-Off, Put-Upon Clerk." Who the hell knew that Georgie Boy was so damn handy?

BRIGHTON BEACH MEMOIRS
(1987)
Director: Gene Saks

The lead actor in this pleasant but all too stagy adaptation of Neil Simon's coming-of-age story set in Brooklyn is none other than Jonathan Silverman of *The Single Guy* fame . . . or infamy. However, the real Must-See performance in *Brighton Beach Memoirs* for

Seinfeld completists comes from Jason Alexander, who also appeared on Broadway in Neil Simon's *Broadway Bound,* a play that is part of the same acclaimed seriocomic theatrical trilogy. Alexander turns up as "Pool Player #1," a pool hustler who has a full head o' hair. The cast for this straight-outta-Brooklyn tale also includes Blythe "Gwyneth Paltrow's Mommy" Danner, Bob Dishy and Judith Ivey and, in a cameo as Mr. Greenblatt, future *Picket Fences* star Fyvush Finkel. *Brighton Beach Memoirs* is highly worthwhile as a play and film, though perhaps no match for *Seinfeld*'s legendary *Rochelle Rochelle.*

PRETTY WOMAN
(1990)
Director: Garry Marshall

No, Jason Alexander doesn't go against type and play the title hooker. However, director Marshall did have one hell of a knack for spotting future *Seinfeld* stars early on. Having already shown the foresight to put Michael Richards in *Young Doctors in Love* as an inept contract killer, Marshall went on to cast Jason Alexander as someone with an even more disreputable profession in this massive Julia Roberts–Richard Gere box-office smash—a lawyer. And he's not only a lawyer, but an arrogant, lying bastard of a lawyer named Philip Stuckey. The stuck-up Stuckey—whose

wife is played by future *Wings* star Amy Yasbeck—is the pit-bullish attorney of Edward Lewis (Gere). Late in the film, Stuckey viciously attacks Vivian Ward (Roberts), who by then has established herself as the world's most adorable "beck and call girl." Not exactly old Georgie Boy's proudest moment. "I was the Scumbag of the United States," Alexander said, describing his brush with jerky jurisprudence to *Rolling Stone*'s Bill Zehme back in 1993. "I struck Julia Roberts." Or as Alexander explained to Peter Tilden in a 1997 *Live!* interview, "I've played my share of assholes."

JACOB'S LADDER
(1990)
Director: Adrian Lyne

A nightmarish, *Twilight Zone*–ish vision with a surprising twist at the end, *Jacob's Ladder* features an effective Tim Robbins performance as Jacob Singer, a tortured Vietnam vet, in a cast that also features Elizabeth Peña, Danny Aiello, Matt Craven and Ving Rhames as well as "Must-See TV" mate Eriq LaSalle, later of *ER,* and even a cameo by Macaulay Culkin. Jason Alexander doesn't appear until quite a ways into the film, when he turns up as a world-weary lawyer named Geary whom Jacob and his platoon go to for help. Without attending a moment of law school,

Alexander has impressively built quite a practice as a respected screen advocate.

WHITE PALACE
(1991)
Director: Luis Mandoki

Perhaps the finest film ever to feature James Spader as a tortured Jewish American Prince, *White Palace* is a strong adaptation of the novel by Glenn Savan, with Spader as Max and Susan Sarandon as Nora, the two players in a dark, unlikely love story full of culture clash and healing. The film prominently features Jason Alexander, with a fairly full head of hair, as Neil David Horowitz, a warm but shallow JAP-y friend of Max. A fashion note: Fans of formal wear should note that Alexander is probably seen more in black tie here than in the entire *Seinfeld* oeuvre.

I DON'T BUY KISSES ANYMORE
(1992)
Director: Mitchell Matovich

Weight Watchers meets minor-league Neil Simon romantic comedy in *I Don't Buy Kisses Anymore,* which pairs Jason Alexander with Nia Peeples, a duo who for reasons that remain unclear have to date failed to become our next Hepburn and Tracy. In a scenario that recalls George Costanza's famed "Sweatpants Speech," Alexander sweetly and subtly plays shoe salesman Bernie Fishbine, whose food issues come to the fore when he falls hard for sociology student Theresa Garabaldi (Peeples) who at first is interested only in surreptitiously studying his eating habits. Why doesn't he just go on a Big Salad diet? Ultimately, *Kisses*—which also features Lainie Kazan, Lou Jacobi, Eileen Brennan and even the great Larry Storch of *F Troop* fame—isn't quite weighty enough for its own good.

THE CONEHEADS
(1993)
Director: Steve Barron

Like *North* (see page 78), the cameo-heavy *Coneheads* represents a rare *Seinfeld* doubleheader—a slightly restrained Richards plays a night clerk at a motel who becomes the first human to meet the Heads. Later Jason Alexander—again with the hairpiece—plays ultrasuburban Larry Farber, the very neighborly neighbor of Beldar and the entire Conehead clan. The rest of the *Coneheads* cast includes Dan Aykroyd, Jane Curtin, Sinbad, Michael McKean, David Spade, Adam Sandler and Jon Lovitz, who—as we all know—would go on to memorably play the faux cancer victim in the *Seinfeld* episode known as "The Scofflaw."

SEINING OFF
JONATHAN KATZ on *Seinfeld*

In Comedy Central's award-winning, insanely funny **Dr. Katz:**
Professional Therapist, *comic, actor and writer Jonathan Katz has found a forum for his dry,*
unique wit that's nearly as perfect as fellow stand-up vets Jerry Seinfeld and Larry David did in
their own comic creation. And really who better to render a professional diagnosis of Seinfeld *than the*
voice of an analyst whose clientele are screwed-up comics?

I started doing stand-up in New York around the time that Seinfeld was sort of moving on to other things, but I got to see him in the early stages of his career. And he was the first guy to cover the audience with a tarp and throw fruit at them. Then he realized he could be just as effective with the observational humor that he does so well.

I would go on at clubs in New York, bomb and then blame it on how stupid the audience was. And then Jerry would go on in front of the same audience and I would realize that it was me that was so stupid. He would do things that were at least as clever if not more, and make them succeed. And I sort of feel the same about his show—*Seinfeld* became the first smart sitcom to succeed in a long time.

This is not even one of his best jokes, but this shows the skill he has. I knew in my heart that there's something funny about life insurance. Then one day I'm watching *The Tonight Show* and he says something like, "Life insurance. Let me see if I get this right—I give you money when I'm alive and then when I die, you give it back to me." But *he* does it funny. It's just finding something that's lying around, and finding what's funny about it.

What was inspiring about what Jerry and Larry did on *Seinfeld* was the way they whittled down a story until it almost isn't there anymore. We try to do the same things on *Dr. Katz: Professional Therapist*—we just make the idea smaller and smaller until we can't remember what it was about.

We had Julia Louis-Dreyfus as a patient on the show—we did it when she was on the phone in her home, very pregnant and being a very good sport. I thought it worked pretty well. I've been asking Larry David for two years to do it—he's married to my ex-manager, among other things. And he was one of the first guys I thought of when we started doing the show because he's such a troubled guy it would be funny.

As for a favorite episode, I always liked the idea of Jerry breaking up with a male friend—I've been there when it just isn't working out. Oddly, when it first started airing the only character who didn't succeed for me was Kramer, and now almost everything he does cracks me up. He's become an acquired taste for me.

BLANKMAN
(1994)
Director: Mike Binder

Even real-life superman Jason Alexander can't do much to save this misguided movie in which Damon Wayans plays a Windy City ghetto superhero who has absolutely no superpowers of which to speak. Also in the *Blankman* cast are David Alan Grier, Robin Givens and, in quite a stretch, Alexander as a bald, crusty wheelchair-bound producer at the sleazy tabloid show called *Hard Edition*. His character is Larry Stone, a sort of gruff Lou Grant-meets-*Ironside*-in-hell, who's known to bark out things like "How's that lesbian necrophiliac story coming?" or "Ratings give me a woody." This is the sort of strong but thankless character acting that no doubt builds character.

NORTH
(1994)
Director: Rob Reiner

There are no doubt dozens of solid reasons for the total box-office failure of *North*—here's one more: Perhaps the world got queasy at the notion of George and Elaine as a couple. A short-cropped Julia Louis-Dreyfus and Jason Alexander play the selfish parents of Rob—The Artist Formerly Known as Meathead—Reiner's adult fairy tale that the whole family could not enjoy

together. As Alexander joked to *Rolling Stone* in 1993, "Actually, we play George and Elaine as if they were husband and wife—the bickering and the simmering sexuality." There are no sex scenes between Louis-Dreyfus and Alexander here, though it couldn't have hurt. Also joining in this star-studded globe-trotting mess are Elijah Wood, Bruce Willis, Dan Aykroyd, Jon Lovitz, Alan Arkin, Kathy Bates, Reba McEntire and Abe Vigoda of *Fish* fame.

THE PAPER
(1994)
Director: Ron Howard

Even if it delivered nothing else, *The Paper*—directed by the onetime Opie—affords filmgoers the chance to enjoy the sight and sound of Alexander saying the word "fuckin'." Additionally, the film offers an entertaining look inside a New York newspaper, with a fine cast including that other Jason, Jason Robards, Michael Keaton, Glenn Close, Randy Quaid and Marisa Tomei, whom George would memorably obsess over in "The Cadillac." Hold those presses, Alexander plays a semi-heavy role as New York City's parking commissioner and drunken lunatic Marion Sandusky who is bent on getting columnist McDougal (Quaid). Apparently Marion is somewhat corrupt, though the worst crime has got to be that scary mustache he's sporting here.

FOR BETTER OR WORSE
(1995)
Director: Jason Alexander

You're a dedicated Georgehead, so you're certain you would have heard of any film directed and starring Jason Alexander, right? Especially one with a cast that includes James Woods, Lolita Davidovich, Beatrice Arthur, Rob Reiner, Joe Mantegna, Jay Mohr, Rip Torn and Steven Wright? Well, think again. *For Better or Worse* is a small movie of mostly small pleasures in which Alexander plays a lonely guy named Michael Makeshift who falls for the girlfriend (Davidovich) of his con-man brother (Woods). The music here features the Bobs, the vocal group Alexander sang with when he cohosted the 1995 Emmy Awards. Alexander's performance is winning as usual, particularly early on, but as the film progresses, his character's last name isn't the only thing that feels a little makeshift.

DUNSTON CHECKS IN
(1996)
Director: Ken Kwapis

A vaguely charming family comedy in the funny-orangutan-in-the-five-star-hotel subgenre, *Dunston Checks In* may leave one with some reservations, but one of them is not the typically fine work by Alexander as Mr. Robert Grant, the manager of the Majestic Hotel. Also in the cast are Faye Dunaway, Paul Reubens, Eric Lloyd, Rupert Everett and, of course, Sam the simian as Dunston. Perhaps in signing on here Alexander noted the success the *Friends* folks had enjoyed with a less evolved costar, despite Matt LeBlanc's hairy brush with *Ed*. A strong, non-Georgian performance from Alexander. *Seinfeld* completists with kids will go positively ape over this hairy tale.

THE LAST SUPPER
(1996)
Director: Stacy Title

Dine on this delicious darkness: *The Last Supper* concerns five liberal grad student housemates in Iowa played by Cameron Diaz, Courtney B. Vance, Annabeth Gish, Jonathan Penner and Ron Eldard who decide to kill those with differing political outlooks. Smaller roles feature Bill Paxton, Mark Harmon, Ron Perlman, Charles Durning and Nora Dunn, as well as Jason Alexander, who has a nicely measured, albeit brief, cameo as a southern anti-environmentalist who becomes a dinner guest of the murderous gang that gets hooked on the big chill. Previously Alexander appeared in an acclaimed short film by director Title (who also happens to be Alexander's sister-in-law) called *Down on the Waterfront*.

LOVE! VALOUR! COMPASSION!
(1997)
Director: Joe Mantello

In a grand yet beautifully understated performance, Jason Alexander plays Buzz Hauser, a Broadway-loving, flamboyantly gay man with AIDS (a role played by Nathan Lane on Broadway) in this solid if underwhelming adaptation of Terrence McNally's play—*not that there's anything wrong with that.* His character is described by another as "the love child of Judy Garland and Liberace." As Alexander told *Today*'s Matt Lauer, he was not especially worried about playing a gay role. "I've never really seen the risk other than I could have been really bad," he said. Of course, he needn't have worried too much. Flesh for fantasy note: Alexander bares his butt here. It's real, and it's fabulous.

The Julia Louis-Dreyfus Oeuvre

HANNAH AND HER SISTERS
(1986)
Director: Woody Allen

More than a decade before *Deconstructing Harry,* Julia Louis-Dreyfus worked with Woody Allen, albeit in a far more limited role. Here she pops up with a vaguely early-Madonna-ish look as a coworker of Mickey (Allen) named Mary. Interestingly, they work together at a *Saturday Night Live*–like sketch comedy show. Her reading of her single line here, "Mickey, we have a half hour to air," is pure genius. Still, in 1997, she too humbly told *Vanity Fair*'s Lloyd Grove, "I had this tiiiiny little part, and I really screwed it up." Of course she did no such thing.

TROLL
(1986)
Director: John Carl Buechler

You better sit down, kids. Few thespians can claim to have worked with both Woody Allen and the late, great Sonny Bono all in one year—talk about dramatic range! This surreally stupid piece of work is one hell of a long way down the food chain from *Hannah,* and almost defies any meaningful description. Okay, I'll try anyway—this is a low-rent *Gremlins* for people who found that flick way too cerebral. As difficult as it may be to believe, the makers of *Troll* intentionally cast future congressman Bono as a swinging single in a cast also featuring a veritable TV all-star team: *Law & Order*'s Michael Moriarty, *Charlie's Angels*' Shelley Hack, *Lost in Space*'s June Lockhart and *WKRP in Cincinnati*'s

Gary Sandy. Louis-Dreyfus plays Jeanette Cooper, apparently a waitress and the girlfriend of William Daniel (played by her real-life hubby, Brad Hall), both of whom pop up fairly early in the film to no great effect as neighbors in a troll-plagued apartment building. Curiously, Louis-Dreyfus failed to sign up for a tour of *Troll II* duty.

SOUL MAN
(1986)
Director: Steve Miner

Movies don't get much more eighties than *Soul Man,* a film that even features the dramatic work of Ron Reagan Jr. Is it social satire or politically correct stupidity? You decide. Still, not even the comic talents of Julia Louis-Dreyfus can make this flick a race/laugh riot. Louis-Dreyfus plays the small role of Lisa Stimson, an ambitious little yuppie and poster child for networking who's a classmate of C. Thomas Howell's character, who fakes being black so he can go to Harvard Law School. Other "soul" brothers and sisters in the cast include Rae Dawn Chong, James Earl Jones, Leslie Nielsen and Ayre Gross.

NATIONAL LAMPOON'S CHRISTMAS VACATION
(1989)
Director: Jeremiah S. Chechik

Xmas: 'tis the season to be schlocky. The third film in the *Vacation* series sees a drop in artistic quality that's less drastic than, say, *Godfather III,* but then again the *Vacation* team wasn't starting from such a lofty perch. An extremely hit-or-miss seasonal send-up, *National Lampoon's Christmas Vacation* stars Chevy Chase, Beverly D'Angelo, Randy Quaid and Julia Louis-Dreyfus, who's given clichéd material to work with as an annoying yuppie neighbor of the Griswold family.

JACK THE BEAR
(1993)
Director: Marshall Herskowitz

Julia Louis-Dreyfus gives a charming and rather straight performance in this Steven Zaillian–penned, Marshall (*thirtysomething*) Herskowitz–directed adaptation of Dan McCall's fine coming-of-age novel, featuring monsters real-life and otherwise. Danny DeVito is the star of the sometimes muddled film, while Louis-Dreyfus effectively plays Peggy Etinger, his sweet associate at a horror show called *Gory News* that DeVito's character hosts. The cast also features Gary Sinise, Andrea Marcovicci and young Robert J. Steinmiller.

SEINING OFF
BOB ODENKIRK on *Seinfeld*

*Bob Odenkirk—who played Ben, Elaine's near-doctor love thing in "The Abstinence"—
is the cofounder of* Mr. Show, *one of the most exciting comedy forces of the nineties. His past credits
include* The Larry Sanders Show, The Ben Stiller Show *and* Saturday Night Live.

Has *Seinfeld* raised the level of comedy on TV? Well, I don't think that's really happened, no. I think *Seinfeld* is at another level of really high quality just as *The Simpsons* is, but I don't think quality influences television much. I don't think people see something of quality and say, "Hey, we should be doing quality work." Because basically *Seinfeld* is a result of a group of smart, funny, genuinely talented people—the actors, the writers, Jerry and Larry David—who went and did the show they wanted. When I was there I have to say it wasn't a lot of fun to do it, partly because everyone's done it for what, eight years? It's not just a job, but it is a job and it didn't seem to have a lot of novelty for them. It's their job and they know what they're doing. They're not coming to work going, "Wow, hey, who are *you*?" I was Julia Louis-Dreyfus's love interest—her one millionth love interest—so it's not like she's going to come to work and go, "What are you about?" People didn't say much to me. They were nice, and they have families now. And Jerry was busy because he was running the show now that Larry David was gone.

I actually got to see Larry David perform. When I went to *Saturday Night Live* in 1987, I would go play the Improv in New York, and he would occasionally be there. I only saw him a few times. He's famous for yelling at the audience and from my perspective he would yell at an audience that hadn't had a chance to know him, or even an audience that would like him. I remember sitting in the back going, Why are you yelling at them? They like you.

By the time I did *Seinfeld,* Jerry was definitely producing that show. He was very busy on rewrites and focusing on every scene, working very hard, long hours. And it pays off, because *everyone* sees that show. I've done a lot of stuff, but it's like nobody's ever seen me until I was on *Seinfeld*. And they still think it's all I've ever done. People will tell me, "Hey, maybe you'll get a break now that you got on that *Seinfeld*. Maybe you'll get to do something on TV."

NORTH
(1994)

See entry in "The Jason Alexander Oeuvre" on page 78.

FATHER'S DAY
(1997)
Director: Ivan Reitman

Father's Day may not be the daddy of all box-office disappointments, but this first big-screen pairing of longtime pals Billy Crystal and Robin Williams was still a pretty big letdown and surprise commercial miss. Julia Louis-Dreyfus is more than up to the decidedly non-neurotic role of Carrie, the wife of Jack Lawrence, the character played by her onetime *Saturday Night Live* colleague Crystal. It's a nicely restrained performance, and Louis-Dreyfus looks lovely—Williams's character Dale Putley is inspired to flirt with her, saying, "May I just say if springtime had a face it would be you." The film—an unnecessary Americanization of the French comedy *Les Compères* that was adapted by the usually dependable Lowell Ganz and Babaloo Mandel—also stars Nastassia Kinski, but in the end that doesn't help much either. Nor does a very punk Mel Gibson cameo. Even with a radiant Louis-Dreyfus, *Father's Day* is no holiday.

DECONSTRUCTING HARRY
(1997)
Director: Woody Allen

More than a decade after turning up all too briefly in *Hannah and Her Sisters*, Julia Louis-Dreyfus takes a more substantial role in Woody Allen's latest profanity-laden exercise in cinematic self-loathing, a biting comedy of too few manners that also stars Allen himself, Kirstie Alley, Judy Davis, Hazelle Goodman, Richard Benjamin, Robin Williams, Eric Bogosian, Amy Irving, Elizabeth Shue, Julie Kavner, Louis-Dreyfus's *Father's Day* screen spouse Billy Crystal and Demi Moore as a born-again Jew. Louis-Dreyfus is in fine form here as Leslie, the slutty fictional sister-in-law who services Richard Benjamin early on. Apparently the original title of *Deconstructing Harry* was *The Worst Man in the World,* which sounds like a great lost *Seinfeld* episode. "I'm older and have more experience under my belt," Dreyfus told *US* magazine's Josh Rottenberg about reteaming with Allen here, "so I was a little less intimidated."

The Michael Richards Oeuvre

YOUNG DOCTORS IN LOVE
(1982)
Director: Garry Marshall

TV giant Garry Marshall (*The Odd Couple, Happy Days*)—who went on to make *Pretty Woman,* not to mention *Exit to Eden*—made his debut as a film director with this mostly brain-dead medical version of an *Airplane* movie—imagine *M*A*S*H* without the war or the wit. Michael Richards appears as Malamud, a klutzy, slapstick-prone hit man for the Mob who talks a little like Kirk Douglas and ends up getting worse than he gives. Doctor's orders: Don't miss the film's timeless dynamite-in-the-bedpan gag. In addition to Richards, *Young Doctors* features a far-flung cast in which you'll also spot Sean Young, Dabney Coleman, Hector Elizondo, Harry Dean Stanton, Patrick Macnee, Taylor Negron, future *Wings* star Crystal Bernard and *Spinal Tap*'s Michael McKean. Also appearing in cameos are a number of soap opera stars of the era including *All My Children*'s Susan Lucci and two actresses from *General Hospital*—Janine Turner and, yes, some actress by the name of Demi Moore.

TRANSYLVANIA 6-5000
(1985)
Director: Rudy DeLuca

The horror! This frightfully unfunny flick is a lunkheaded low-rent *Young Frankenstein*-ish spoof that wastes the talents of not only Michael Richards, but also Jeff Goldblum, Carol Kane (who it should be remembered also appears briefly in the *Seinfeld* episode "The Conversion"), Geena Davis, Jeffrey Jones and the great Norman "Mr. Roper" Fell. Despite the second-rate nature of the context, Richards throws himself fully into playing Fejos—an Igor/butler for the Transylvanian hotel who has a heavy accent. *Transylvania 6-5000* is funny only in small bites and scary primarily as a waste of talent.

WHOOPS APOCALYPSE
(1986)
Director: Tom Bussmann

A justifiably obscure political comedy in which Loretta Swit (who'd most notably starred as Major Margaret "Hot Lips" Houlihan on the *M*A*S*H* series) plays America's first female president, Barbara Adams, desperately trying to stop nuclear war despite her wacky staff. Michael Richards can be found here in an international supporting cast that also includes the likes of Peter

Cook, Ian Richardson, Rick Mayall, Alexei Sayle, Daniel Benzali and *Pink Panther* veteran Herbert Lom. Richards plays Lacrobat, the world's worst terrorist and a man of many disguises. Based on a British TV series, this is a transcontinental mess of a movie. Still, for Al Jolson–loving Kramerheads, it's a rare chance to see Richards in blackface.

UHF
(1989)
Director: Jay Levey

An attempted cinematic crossover move for popular pop music parodist "Weird Al" Yankovic, *UHF* is a small-screen send-up that finds Yankovic playing George Newman, who goes from burger flipper to programming genius. The cast includes Victoria Jackson, Billy Barty, Emo Phillips, Fran Drescher, Anthony Geary and Michael Richards, who plays Stanley Spadowsky, a dumb, buck-toothed moron who's fired as a janitor, then quickly hired by Al as the host of *Stanley Spadowsky's Clubhouse* on channel 62. As in *Airheads* (see page 86), not even Richards can clean up this particular pop-cultural mess.

PROBLEM CHILD
(1990)
Director: Dennis Dugan

A horribly crude, wannabe wacky adoption yarn with John Ritter, Michael

Oliver, future *Wing*ster Amy Yasbeck (who was married to Jason Alexander's character in *Pretty Woman*), Gilbert Gottfried and Michael Richards as Martin Beck, a.k.a. the "Fiend of the Century" or the "Bow Tie Killer"—a sadistic mass murderer who becomes a hero to the adopted bad seed. Mass murderers and kids—now *that's* a funny combination. *Problem Child* is the sort of overly broad dreck that has one yearning for the relative subtlety of a *Fridays* sketch. A bomb that not even a *Seinfeld* star can upgrade significantly.

THE CONEHEADS
(1993)

See entry in "The Jason Alexander Oeuvre" on page 76.

SO I MARRIED AN AXE MURDERER
(1993)
Director: Thomas Schlamme

Yes, Virginia, there *was* life before *Austin Powers,* though there's not quite enough life in this intermittently entertaining Mike Myers vehicle, which also features the talents of Nancy Travis, Anthony LaPaglia, Amanda Plummer and—in a brief cameo—Michael Richards as a rather strange man who works in the obituary department of the *San Francisco Globe.* The character is vaguely Krameresque but to little effect. On the adolescent upside, you do get to hear Richards say "Shit."

AIRHEADS
(1994)
Director: Michael Lehmann

Oh, how the mighty director of *Heathers* has fallen here. Michael Richards's character, Doug Beech, spends much of this empty-headed film in an air shaft, while Richards the actor spends most of the movie in slapstick hell. The appropriately titled *Airheads* is a mediocre metalhead mess of a comedy about a band called the Lone Rangers who take KPPX, a Los Angeles radio station, hostage. Also taking part here are Brendan Fraser, Joe Mantegna, Adam Sandler, Steve Buscemi and the late Chris Farley. Richards plays a nervous, mustached station bureaucrat who spends much of the movie hiding in the station's air-conditioning vent systems. By the movie's end, you will feel similarly trapped.

UNSTRUNG HEROES
(1995)
Director: Diane Keaton

The massive talent and range of Michael Richards finally connects with a film that actually deserves him. Based on an autobiographical book by Franz Lidz, *Unstrung Heroes* captures what it's like for a young boy (Nathan Watt) growing up with a decidedly quirky family in sixties Los Angeles. Richards makes a wildly Krameresque entrance as Danny Lidz, an eccentric, paranoid character who along with brother Arthur (Maury Chaykin) takes in the boy who's the son of Selma Lidz (Andie MacDowell) and Sid Lidz (John Turturro). *Unstrung Heroes* gives Richards a chance to be his usual hilarious self, and at the same time explore the more serious side of the benevolent and bemusing insanity that he brings to so many of his characters.

TRIAL AND ERROR
(1997)
Director: Jonathan Lynn

Jurisprudence takes a mildly wacky holiday in this sometimes amusing comedy that stars Michael Richards as an out-of-work actor who ends up covering for his lawyer buddy (Jeff Daniels) by improvising as an attorney in a case defending a con man played by *Larry Sanders*'s great Rip Torn. The ultimate verdict about *Trial and Error* is that there's a whole lot of talent on display in this more litigious and only slightly smarter *Dumb & Dumber*.

SEINING OFF
BRUCE MAHLER on *Seinfeld*

Bruce Mahler played the hilarious and controversial loose-lipped rabbi who gets
Elaine in trouble in "The Postponement" and reappeared briefly in "The Serenity Now." Mahler met
Seinfeld *cocreator Larry David doing stand-up in New York in the seventies, and later, in the early*
eighties, he was a cast member on Fridays *with both Larry David and Michael Richards.*

Let me tell you the genesis of the rabbi. I'm sitting in my apartment years and years ago when we're doing *Fridays*, and an old girlfriend is holding a piece of matzo and I accidentally snapped it in two. And I said, "It's funny, it's almost like a Jewish version of kung fu." I ran in to *Fridays* and said to Larry, "I have a great idea for these two rabbis," and we put together a sketch that got on for that particular episode called "Matzoid," a self-defense program with us as these two pathetically bad rabbis. Emmanuel Kimmelman was my guy, and Isaiah Feinberg was Larry's. That led to cooking shows and other scenarios. Then the idea almost died, but then it got revived by one of the other writers on *Fridays* who helped us do a thing called "Enter the Matzoid" down in Chinatown. It was kind of a Bruce Lee thing—we were going to call the guy Bruce Leibowitz, but we didn't. At that point Larry came in and we wrote some great things at *Fridays,* like a James Bond parody called "You Should Only Live Twice." We fought GOYIM—the Global Organization of Young Irrational Maniacs. We also did a take-off on *That's Incredible* called *That's Meshugina.*

Here's a little-known Larry David story. *Fridays* was a live show, and when the first "Matzoid" thing went on the air we were one minute to air, and both of us were so nervous and had to piss like racehorses. I said, "Look, we have a responsibility here to give the best performance, and if we have full bladders we won't give a great performance." So we peed backstage on the floor, and went out and did a great show, and thereafter I think it became a good luck symbol.

Larry's done a number of Jewish sketches. He just called and said, "Do that guy but in a new context. Do that rabbi voice." It's a little different—the rabbi characters were two people. But Larry knew I could do that. This guy in *Seinfeld* is a bit of a gossip, he didn't handle secrets well. I taped a little scene lurking in a doorway listening to Elaine or something, but it ended up on the cutting room floor. I'm very sorry to say that episode generated more angry mail from Jews—let's call it Angry Jew Mail—than any of the other episodes they did. I think because of that the character did not come back for a while. But why can't a rabbi be a gossip? Jesus Christ, if a child molester can be a Ph.D., then a rabbi can be a gossip too.

SEINFELD AND THE GREAT NINETIES NEW YORK REVIVAL
An Argument for Comic Cause and Actual Effect

What James Joyce did for Dublin, what Bruce Springsteen did for the Garden State, *Seinfeld* has done for the Upper West Side specifically and for the greater New York City area in general. As someone who lived close to the rotten core of the Big Apple for most of my life, and foolishly fled to the Wild West just as *Seinfeld* was really getting under way, I can personally attest to the remarkable change in the city that is manifest in the P.S. era—Post-*Seinfeld*, that is. Thanks in part to all the good work of Jerry, George, Elaine and Kramer, New York City has become a boomtown of the first order all over again. Real estate values have soared, crime is down and the image of the city has improved, possibly because the masses of *Seinfeld* followers have wrongly concluded that

> "Right now New York is the most popular city in the world. You can't believe this town. I don't know that Jerry wants to leave California, but I'd love it if he did."
>
> —*George Steinbrenner*

one could behave just as irresponsibly and bizarrely as Cosmo Kramer and still somehow afford to live in a very nice building on the Upper West Side.

"That's not a far reach," says George Steinbrenner when offered this view of *Seinfeld*'s contribution to the city's fortunes. "It's all part of New York, even the Soup Nazi. And they *have* captured some of New York. I don't think it hurts at all—it helps New York. And I think New York is proud of them. They pick some of the extremes, but that's what makes New York such a great city. And right now New York is the most popular city in the world. You can't believe this town. I don't know that Jerry wants to leave California, but I'd love it if he did." (All indications are that Jerry's coming home from La La Land.)

Former mayor—and current *People's Court* judge—Ed Koch agrees. As Hizzoner said, "Has

Seinfeld helped turn around New York? Oh, *sure*, I think it's a very positive statement for turning around people who might have a misconception about New Yorkers."

All right, maybe there were a few other annoying socioeconomic factors in the rallying of New York City during the nineties, but I'll leave those ponderables to other theorists. For the sake of argument, I prefer to give all the credit for this turnaround to *Seinfeld*. Though the series is largely shot on a soundstage in Studio City, California—with the cast accordingly based in L.A. much of the year—*Seinfeld* has probably done more to add luster to the Big Apple than at least a few of the city's recent mayoral administrations. And arguably, it took the Costanzas to make Queens hip. Before *Seinfeld*, the general consensus was that TV shows ought to take place in a more generalized American setting, one more easy to relate to for all those annoying non–New Yorkers out there in the cable-ready heartland. Today there are twenty prime-time series set in New York.

Seinfeld has helped turn New York City from a punch line in jokes about crime to a hotbed of glamour and laughs. In the Must-See world of TV, *Seinfeld* to some degree begot *Friends,* which in turn appeared to beget dozens of either faux New York shows or shows that actually dared to be shot there, like *Spin City*. Such was the political clout of the *Seinfeld* vote that renowned funnyman Rudy Giuliani popped up—briefly, thankfully—in "The Non-Fat Yogurt" while George Steinbrenner became a big TV star, albeit in an off-camera form.

Certainly years before *Seinfeld* there had been other massively successful shows set in the New York area, such as *The Honeymooners* and *All in the Family* and *Cosby*. But *Seinfeld* deserves thanks for taking the masses straight into the bagel-heavy heart of a certain distinctly Manhattan milieu, a strange land of bad parking, gabby rabbis, disgruntled postal workers and some very odd characters who could live and in their pitiful way thrive only in New York City.

Mommie Dearest: George with the
mother of all mothers.

MULTIPLE MISHAGAS

1. Which popular periodical is George pleasuring himself to when his mother catches him in the act in "The Contest"?
   a. *Guns & Ammo*
   b. *Modern Maturity*
   c. *Glamour*
   d. *The New Yorker*

2. In what TV movie has Jason Alexander starred?
   a. *Winds of War*
   b. *Bye Bye Birdie*
   c. *Rochelle Rochelle: The TV Movie*
   d. *Love, Valour, Compassion*

3. What's the name of the fake game show hosted by Jerry Seinfeld in a sketch on Saturday Night Live?
   a. *Stand-Up and Win*
   b. *Who's the Jew?*
   c. *Single, Thin & Neat*
   d. *Who Are These People?*

4. Which of the following products has not been endorsed by one of the main Seinfeld stars?
   a. American Express
   b. Rold Gold pretzels
   c. Nice 'N' Easy hair coloring
   d. Depends adult diapers

5. Sheree North—who plays Kramer's mom, Babs, in "The Switch"—had a recurring role in which of these classic sitcoms?
   a. *The Mary Tyler Moore Show*
   b. *Mr. Rhodes*
   c. *Taxi*
   d. *The Jeffersons*

6. Which of the following pop songs can Newman be heard singing in "The Pothole"?
   a. "Davy the Fat Boy" by Randy Newman
   b. "Please Mr. Postman" by the Marvelettes
   c. "Three Times a Lady" by the Commodores
   d. "Eat to the Beat" by Blondie

7. *You will* not *find Jerry Stiller, who plays Mr. Frank Costanza on* Seinfeld, *in which of the following movies?*
   a. *The Boys from Brazil*
   b. *The Taking of Pelham One Two Three*
   c. *Awakenings*
   d. *Rapa Nui*

8. *Which of the following is* not *a magazine that Jerry Seinfeld's photo has graced the cover of to date?*
   a. *Business Week*
   b. *Buck Naked*
   c. *Rolling Stone*
   d. *Automobile*

9. *Which of these singers of the new wave era played George's relative Shelly in "The Contest"?*
   a. Patti Smith
   b. Patty Smyth
   c. Rachel Sweet
   d. Elvis Costello

10. *What was the real name of the New York restaurant on which "The Soup Nazi" is apparently based?*
   a. The Soup Fascist
   b. The Soup Kitchen International
   c. Führer's Favorite Foodstuffs
   d. The Master Race Bar and Grill

11. *Which of the following is* not *a TV show on which Michael Richards has appeared?*
   a. *Scarecrow and Mrs. King*
   b. *Hill Street Blues*
   c. *Singled Out*
   d. *St. Elsewhere*

12. *What was the name of the character Julia Louis-Dreyfus played in the late-eighties NBC sitcom* Day by Day?
   a. Eileen Swift
   b. Daisy Buchanan
   c. Elaine Dennis
   d. Ishmael

13. *What was Jason Alexander's first school play?*
   a. *Bye Bye Birdie*
   b. *The Sound of Music*
   c. *Two Gentlemen from Pomona*
   d. *Hair*

14. *Which* Seinfeld *actor won Emmys for Supporting Actor in a Comedy Series for both the 1992–1993 and 1993–1994 seasons?*
   a. Jason Alexander
   b. Michael Richards
   c. Jerry Seinfeld
   d. Wayne Knight

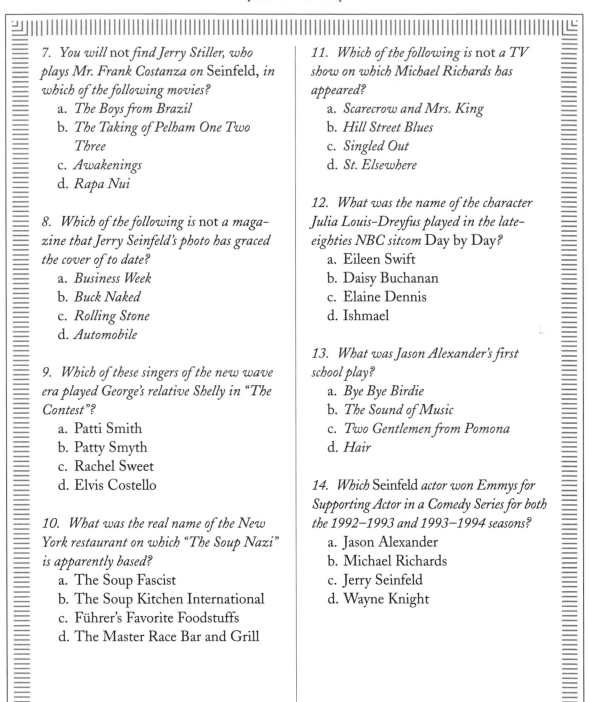

SEINING OFF
MARY HART on *Seinfeld*

The leggy Entertainment Tonight *anchor achieved* Seinfeld*ian fame when her familiar voice gave Kramer seizures in "The Good Samaritan" episode. For the record, this author experienced no medical reaction during the following conversation with this hostess with* E.T.'s *mostest.*

Were you proud to have evoked such a strong reaction from Kramer?

Well, first of all the episode is hysterical. I have personally done some episodic TV, so I know when things rerun. Never had I heard reports of anything rerunning as many times as that particular episode. It made *such* a mark. At first it was a little bit of a shock, but I agreed with everybody—it was a wonderfully funny episode. I just wish I had that impact on Kramer every time I talk to him. I'm absolutely a fan of the show. I can't say I've ever had a seizure watching *Seinfeld*, but you know even though they deal with things that afflict people on a daily basis, they turn them into such humorous incidents that a good laugh is healthy for everybody. I think *Seinfeld* has absolutely had a huge impact on television. I remember when it first went on, and we kept saying, "Here's the show about nothing that's number one again."

There's a reason that cast negotiated to stay together, and they were smart to do so, because without one of the parts it wouldn't be the same. They're all such incredibly talented people and together they're gangbusters. Every once in a while I really do run into Michael Richards and I keep expecting him to go into spasms, but it hasn't happened yet.

15. *To date, which of the following is* not *the title of a* Seinfeld *episode?*
   a. "The Curious Cantor"
   b. "The Bris"
   c. "The Rye"
   d. "The Sniffing Accountant"

16. *Besides his familiar* Seinfeld *theme, Jonathan Wolff has scored music for all the following shows, except which one?*
   a. *21 Jump Street*
   b. *Married . . . With Children*
   c. *Homeboys from Outer Space*
   d. *Who's the Boss?*

SEINING OFF
TERI HATCHER on *Seinfeld*

Television's Lois Lane of Lois & Clark—The New Adventures of Superman *gave a superheroic performance in "The Implant" as Sidra, the statuesque beauty whose chest drives Jerry to distraction when he decides he must know whether two of her prominent attributes are real or not. In the end, Sidra famously walks out on Jerry right after letting him know that they're real and they're fabulous. As Hatcher makes clear here, her love for the fabulous* Seinfeld *is also very real.*

People coming up to me and saying, "They're real and they're fabulous"—that lasted for a couple years there. For a while, that was the intro to almost every conversation I had.

When I think about work and success, I sometimes think in terms of effort put in. And I'm telling you that *Seinfeld* was the most minimal effort in my career. It was the nicest set I've ever worked on, and the least amount of hours with a bunch of brilliantly funny people. The whole thing was so effortless that it's unbelievable how much notice came from doing that one episode.

Way before I did it, *Seinfeld* was my favorite show on television. I don't watch a lot of television—I watch the Discovery Channel, CNN and old movies. One thing that Jerry was extremely smart about is that he didn't have a lot of ego and possessiveness about it being *his* show. He was really generous to these three other great actors to give them fabulous, rich characters and so many funny lines. So in the end they all complement one another. And I also think Larry David is just so brilliant.

I don't take any credit for how funny that episode is. It could have been any pretty, funny actress and it just happened to be me.

---

17. Which United States President did Jason Alexander play on the Los Angeles stage?
   a. James Buchanan
   b. Richard Nixon
   c. Harry Truman
   d. William Henry Harrison

18. Who of the following has never directed an episode of Seinfeld?
   a. Andy Ackerman
   b. Jason Alexander
   c. Tom Cherones
   d. James Cameron

19. What famous comedian has Michael Richards credited with giving him an important early break?
    a. Billy Crystal
    b. Slappy White
    c. Jacques Tati
    d. Foster Brooks

20. In 1997, who did Regis Philbin mention to Jason Alexander as being the other great supporting TV character actor of all time besides Jason himself?
    a. Dorothy "Tootie" Ramsey in *The Facts of Life*
    b. Dr. Bernie Tupperman in *The Bob Newhart Show*
    c. Jimmy Osmond in *Donny and Marie*
    d. Ed Norton in *The Honeymooners*

21. In which Sondheim musical did Jason Alexander make his Broadway debut?
    a. *Company*
    b. *Merrily We Roll Along*
    c. *Sweeney Todd*
    d. *Into the Woods*

22. What character did Jason Alexander provide the voice for on the animated Duckman *series*?
    a. Fluffy
    b. Mambo
    c. Cornfed
    d. Duckman

23. In SeinLanguage, *Jerry Seinfeld says when he was growing up he was the only young person in his neighborhood to have all the albums of which of the following recording acts?*
    a. Bobby Vinton
    b. Mantovani
    c. Bill Cosby
    d. The Sex Pistols

24. Who plays Michael Richards's lawyer buddy in the film Trial and Error?
    a. Gregory Peck
    b. Jeff Daniels
    c. Paul Newman
    d. Christopher Darden

25. Julia Louis-Dreyfus got into a much publicized parking space altercation with which of the following TV personalities back in 1992?
    a. Tom Arnold
    b. ALF
    c. Wayne Knight
    d. Ted Koppel

26. What was the title of the 1987 sitcom in which Jason Alexander played the co-owner of a products-testing company?
    a. *Curious George*
    b. *The Single Testing Guy*
    c. *Make Room for Schleppo*
    d. *Everything's Relative*

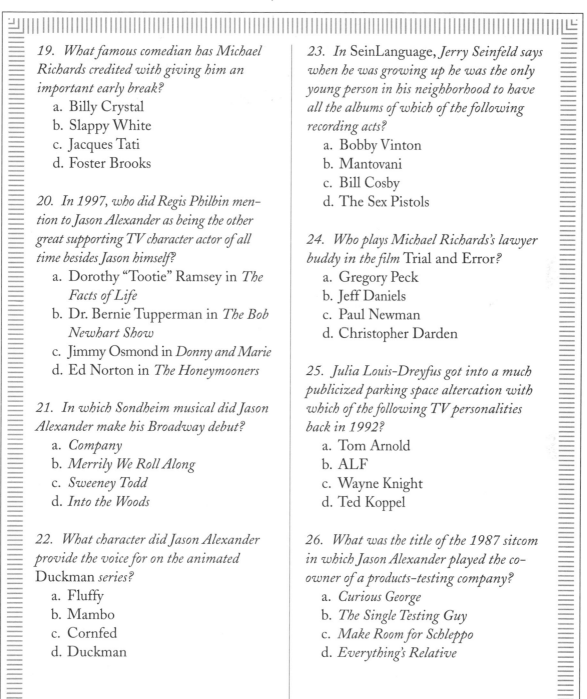

I
SING
THE
BODY
SEINFELD

The Evolution of the Series

Over the course of nine historic seasons for sustained hysterics, we have watched proudly as *Seinfeld*'s fab four have grown up before our very eyes—from a bunch of bonded misfits and screwups into a bunch of bonded misfits and screwups who

were nine seasons older. Even if that old gang of ours didn't make any great strides forward in the maturity department, the show itself has continued to evolve in intriguing ways, always finding a new way to surprise us by pushing the comedic envelope. Each season had its own character—and indeed its own characters—as well as its own highs and lows. But the highs were incredibly high and, come to

> ## "Therefore all seasons shall be sweet to thee."
>
> —Samuel Taylor Coleridge, *who tragically was too ancient a mariner to watch any of the seasons of* Seinfeld

think of it, the lows were pretty damn high too, at least in this humble critic's opinion. What follows, then, is an extended look at the ascent of man as seen and ridiculed in the inspired oeuvre groove of *Seinfeld*. Programming note: Double episodes are listed as one, and "best of," retrospective episodes are ignored like Bania was.

THE FIRST SEASON

1. THE SEINFELD CHRONICLES
Initial Airdate: July 5, 1989

The mother of all *Seinfeld*s, *The Seinfeld Chronicles*—apparently also known as *Good News, Bad News*—was a pilot originally not picked up. Seeing this episode now becomes a truly "Bizarro Jerry" experience for the *Seinfeld* lover. First of all, we get no Elaine here but some less interesting waitress, and a Kramer who's not quite the nutcase we've all come to know and sort of love. Directed by one Art Wolfe, this episode finds Jerry wondering about the intentions of a female out-of-town guest. For a show that was soon to change the world, this initial salvo feels a little conventional.

....

2. THE STAKEOUT
Initial Airdate: May 31, 1990

The second time around, in "The Stakeout," things grow significantly closer to a recognizable *Seinfeld* reality. Much mirth is made here regarding the lighter side of stalking when Jerry becomes so interested in a woman he meets that he decides to stake her out at her place of work. The always-captivating Julia Louis-Dreyfus makes her debut in this episode as Jerry's former flame Elaine Benes. "The Stakeout" was historically significant as the first *Seinfeld* episode to feature Jonathan Wolff's familiar theme music. This groundbreaking episode also boasts the first mention of George Costanza's renaissance-man alter ego, Art Vandelay.

In "The Stakeout," we meet Jerry's mom, Helen Seinfeld (Liz Sheridan). What's the name of the actor—since replaced by Barney Martin—who originally played Jerry's dad in this episode?
  a. Phil Bruns
  b. Alan King
  c. Soupy Sales
  d. Jason Robards

SEINING OFF
MOLLY SHANNON on *Seinfeld*

A standout talent in the current Saturday Night Live *cast, Shannon is perhaps best known for her awkward Catholic schoolgirl character Mary Katherine Gallagher, and for playing one hell of a Court-ney Love. She also made a vivid impression as Elaine's nemesis/colleague Sam—she of the unusual walk—in the "Summer of George" episode that ended the eighth season of* Seinfeld.

It was *great* doing *Seinfeld*, especially since I'm a huge fan of the show. Steven Koren and Dave Mandel, who are writers on *Seinfeld*, used to be on *Saturday Night Live*, so they're the ones who brought me in on it. Still I had to audition for it, so I was out there for a week off from our show. I hadn't auditioned in a while so I was kind of bummed. I went in and there were all these girls—they always have the best girls audition for that show. Watching them work was so much fun—I'd say it was so fluid because they have such a good time and trust themselves. They're really a team. Jerry likes you to trust yourself too, so if I got too neurotic or needy, he would be like, "You know it's fine." After the episode aired, I got *tons* of reaction—I was like, "Holy shit." The response you get from being on *Seinfeld* is just unbelievable. I do late-night TV, and the difference between late-night TV and that show is incredible. Everybody watches *Seinfeld*. It's like an explosion. I still get people coming up to me about that character. In terms of my own favorite episodes, I love the masturbation episode—that one's hard to beat.

3. THE ROBBERY
Initial Airdate: June 7, 1990

Calling "The Robbery" criminally amusing might be overstating matters just a bit, but this was an episode that helped establish some of the hilarious selfishness and immaturity that would become dysfunctional hallmarks of the enduring *Seinfeld* zeitgeist. Jerry's apartment is robbed, despite his acquisition of the impenetrable Klatco D-29 lock, and then realtor George finds him a new dream pad, a dream George soon aspires to have for himself. In the end, of course, neither of them nor Elaine gets the real estate upgrade they so desire.

4. MALE UNBONDING
Initial Airdate: June 14, 1990

"Male Unbonding" offers an early hint that the *Seinfeld* view of friendship will have an appealing edge, as Jerry tries to figure out how the hell to lose an old pal of whom he's grown weary, while Georgie Boy—go figure—has some relationship trouble of his own. And in the distinguished tradition of fellow schemer-dreamer Ralph Kramden, Kramer launches the first of many get-rich schemes to come.

Which of these actors plays Jerry's pal Joel whom he decides to shake off in "Male Unbonding"?
   a. Kevin Dunn
   b. Kevin Kline
   c. Kevin Bacon
   d. Kevin Costner

5. THE STOCK TIP
Initial Airdate: June 21, 1990

Seinfeld meets *Wall Street* in "The Stock Tip"—one of the lesser scripts penned by Jerry Seinfeld and Larry David—and the result is still a lot funnier than your average Oliver Stone flick. Unusually, the oft-losing George manages to make a little fiscal killing in the end. There's also a heavy-petting problem here, as Elaine loses out on love because of some furry competition. Jerry and girlfriend Vanessa (Lynn Clark) have a less than idyllic Vermont trip.

THE SECOND SEASON

6. THE EX-GIRLFRIEND

Initial Airdate: January 23, 1991

What's a little love interest–swapping among friends, especially when neither pal actually likes the woman in question? George's Southern Gothic gal pal Marlene (Tracy Kolis) exerts some sort of odd psychosexual power over Jerry in this particularly strong episode from David and Seinfeld, but eventually she loses interest in our stand-up guy after she sees his act. As Mrs. Seinfeld herself might ask—and will pretty damn soon—how could anybody *not* like him?

7. THE PONY REMARK

Initial Airdate: January 30, 1991

It's a darkly funny family affair when Jerry's casual equestrian put-down coincides uncomfortably closely with the death of Manya (Rozsika Halmos), an elderly Seinfeld family matriarch. In the David and Seinfeld–penned "The Pony Remark," we hear about some characters who will be much remarked on though little seen in the future: Uncle Leo mentions the supposed family success story Cousin Jeffrey, and Kramer discusses the soon to be mythic Bob Sacamano. Guilt plagues Jerry here, but true to *Seinfeld* form—where a strict statute of limitations seems to exist on any such responsible and adult feelings—he soon gets over it.

Which of the following actors plays Uncle Leo, the highly annoying and annoyed character who makes his first of many unpleasant appearances in the family-oriented "The Pony Remark"?
   a. Len Lesser
   b. Pat Cooper
   c. Pat Morita
   d. Fred Savage

8. THE JACKET

Initial Airdate: February 6, 1991

It's daddy dearest time at *Seinfeld* in "The Jacket," a stylish episode that should prove especially illuminating to developmental psychiatrists wanting a fairly good hint as to why Elaine is screwed up—at least screwed up enough to hang out so much with Jerry and the guys. Wait for "The Jacket" to pop up in syndication and take the less than pleasant opportunity to meet Elaine's posturing pop, Alton Benes (Lawrence Tierney), an extremely crusty, Hemingwayesque writer who definitely doesn't take a shine to his daughter's less manly pals. Subtitle this one "The Old Man and the Wimps."

In "The Jacket," George gets a song from which of the following musicals stuck in his head?

　　a. *Springtime for Hitler*
　　b. *Les Misérables*
　　c. *Nunsense*
　　d. *Titanic*

9. THE PHONE MESSAGE
Initial Airdate: February 13, 1991

Many years before such comedic territory was fruitfully explored in *Swingers*, *Seinfeld* brilliantly documented the dangers of contemporary phone machine etiquette in "The Phone Message," an episode in which George blows his big chance with a woman and then comically compounds his error over the phone. And in a sign of things to come over and over again, Jerry has a relationship end for fantastically insignificant reasons—this time conflicting feelings regarding a particular Dockers commercial.

10. THE APARTMENT
Initial Airdate: April 4, 1991

Certain pivotal events are burned forever into the collective consciousness of mankind. The discovery of fire, say, or the invention of the lightbulb. In the case of "The Apartment," it's the birth of Elaine's enthusiastic "Get out!" exclamation—truly a life-affirming phrase for the ages, uttered here for the first of many times to come. Penned by Peter Mehlman, the episode finds Kramer moussing that famous head o' hair and George using a wedding band to attract women.

11. THE STATUE
Initial Airdate: April 11, 1991

Unfortunately "The Statue"—written by the usually trusty Larry Charles—is a tad too stationary for its own comedic good. Rava—a darkly exotic authoress whose work Elaine edits at Pendant Publishing—has an oddly pretentious boyfriend named Ray who does a bang-up job as a housekeeper for Jerry. That is, until Jerry thinks he can't trust Ray.

In "The Statue," Elaine's gloomy writer Rava hails from which of the following countries?

    a. Fredonia
    b. Israel
    c. Finland
    d. Burma

12. THE REVENGE
Initial Airdate: April 18, 1991

A self-inflicted career crisis for status-conscious George, and a slowly unfolding laundromat drama for Jerry and Kramer mark the only semi-sweet "The Revenge." This is not an especially lasting *Seinfeld* episode, though George's charming brand of rationalized insanity is beginning to come into wonderfully close focus here, as we see him trying to rectify one of his too-numerous-to-count professional disasters.

Topic for further discussion: Why is Elaine so glad to assist George in slipping his former boss a mickey?

13. THE HEART ATTACK
Initial Airdate: April 25, 1991

Laughter is supposedly the best medicine, but there's not quite enough curing going on in "The Heart Attack." The unlucky thirteenth episode of *Seinfeld*, this turns into a bit of a medical mess, as George believes he's had a heart attack yet decides to cut corners by following Kramer's second opinion and going with the advice of a slightly nutty and ultimately harmful holistic healer played by veteran character actor Stephen Tobolowsky.

Which of the following shows did the nutty healer Stephen Tobolowsky not *appear in?*

    a. *Dweebs*
    b. *Whole New Ball Game*
    c. *South Park*
    d. *Blue Skies*

14. THE DEAL
Initial Airdate: May 2, 1991

"The Deal" deals with a little sexual healing. Now, for all their problems, the *Seinfeld* gang get their share of coitus, but generally not with one another. Turned on by the TV, Jerry and Elaine reheat their old affair with surprising results. This is an early example of *Seinfeld*'s graceful dance around censorship matters—the words *this* and *that* have never sounded so sexually loaded as they do here.

Siobhan Fallon, who plays Elaine's annoy-ing, free-spirited roommate in "The Deal," appeared on what popular comedy show?

   a. *Saturday Night Live*
   b. *Your Show of Shows*
   c. *Mad TV*
   d. *Jerry Springer*

Topic for further discussion: What do you think Jerry and Elaine's offspring would look like?

15. THE BABY SHOWER
Initial Airdate: May 16, 1991

In the tradition of the great W. C. Fields, *Seinfeld* has always taken a politi-cally incorrect and somewhat jaundiced view of children. "The Baby Shower"—written by Larry Charles—is proof pos-itive that *Seinfeld* is no kids' show, as Elaine throws a baby shower in Jerry's apartment for a friend. Meanwhile, Jerry endures some extreme cable guy prob-lems years before *The Cable Guy*. As can happen with any such infantile affair, this "Baby Shower" is fun but goes on a little long.

Which of these actors plays the illegal cable guy in "The Baby Shower"?

   a. Jim Carrey
   b. Sir John Gielgud
   c. Vic Polizos
   d. Matt Damon

16. THE CHINESE RESTAURANT
Initial Airdate: May 23, 1991

The only problem with "The Chinese Restaurant" is that an hour later, you'll want to feast on it all over again. This is the sort of appetizing episode that's not so much about nothing as it is about something small but real that's perfectly and very artfully rendered. Jerry, George and Elaine head to dinner at a Chinese restaurant so they can grab a quick pre-movie meal, but as it turns out, satisfac-tion is not on the menu in this brilliantly written (by Larry David and Seinfeld) and acted show. "The Chinese Restau-rant" offers all this fun and absolutely no MSG.

What movie is the gang trying to get to see when they get waylaid in "The Chinese Restaurant"?

   a. *Plan 9 from Outer Space*
   b. *Chinatown*
   c. *After Hours*
   d. *North*

SEINING OFF
CRAIG KILBORN on *Seinfeld*

*Craig Kilborn—who first made a splash with his wise-ass commentary on
ESPN's Sports Center—is the highly amusing host of Comedy Central's The Daily Show.
He passed on these reflections on Seinfeld.*

George . . . Lovable, sensitive, understanding . . . He's none of these things. George is every man you'd never want to be.

Kramer . . . Reminds me a lot of myself. He's tall and chicks seem to dig him . . . although nobody really knows why.

Elaine . . . I'd prefer not to comment on women I've slept with (see George's mother).

Jerry . . . What can you say except I've lost a sock in the dryer too.

17. THE BUSBOY
Initial Airdate: June 26, 1991

Here's a generous comedy tip: "The Busboy" is not an episode worth waiting on compared to the show's usual excellent fare. George accidentally gets the title character fired, then makes a greater mess of things. Elaine—who will host her share of bums over the years—has a houseguest who stays too long, which is sort of like how "The Busboy" comes to feel. Usually, *Seinfeld* provides service with a lot more smiles than it does here, in one of Larry David and Jerry Seinfeld's less tasty treats.

THE THIRD SEASON

18. THE NOTE

Initial Airdate: September 18, 1991

A relatively touchy-feely episode by *Seinfeld* standards, the season-opening "The Note" is most noteworthy for the too-exciting massage that sets off George's full-blown psychosexual neurosis. Jason Alexander's portrayal of George's gender insecurities is good, neurotic fun. Jerry gets in trouble when it's revealed that a dentist is getting him free massages. Star sighting: Kramer believes he sees Joe DiMaggio at Dinky Donuts.

What team that Joe DiMaggio played for figures most prominently in future Seinfeld *episodes?*
   a. The Monroe Skirts
   b. The Brooklyn Dodgers
   c. The Los Angeles Dodgers
   d. The New York Yankees

19. THE TRUTH

Initial Airdate: September 25, 1991

There's nothing taxing about "The Truth," in which George is in fine, neurotic form as he destroys the pretentious

Patrice (*Northern Exposure*'s Valerie Mahaffey), a Thomas Carlyle–quoting former IRS employee who is to help out Jerry with an audit before her untimely breakdown. Elaine has problems with her roommate's love life. Notable in this episode directed by famed stand-up David Steinberg is Jerry's vaguely Mob-like outfit during his stand-up bit.

What character did Valerie Mahaffey play in Northern Exposure*?*
   a. D.J. Chris Stevens
   b. Shelley the waitress
   c. The Alaskan Soup Nazi
   d. Eve the hypochondriac

20. THE PEN

Initial Airdate: October 2, 1991

Could *Seinfeld* have helped make south Florida hip again? In "The Pen," Jerry and Elaine head down to soak up a few rays in Florida with Morty and Helen Seinfeld. Elaine becomes temporarily disabled by a bad bed in the Seinfeld home, and Jerry makes the mistake of accepting an astronaut pen. This is a rare episode in which we don't see two members of our comic fab four, but that doesn't stop "The Pen"—written by Larry David—from becoming indelible.

"The Pen" marks the Seinfeld *debut of veteran comedian Sandy Baron as Seinfeld neighbor and sometime nemesis Jack Klompus, who gives Jerry the astronaut pen. Which of the following is* not *a TV show on which Baron has appeared in the past?*

    a. *Hey Landlord*
    b. *That Was the Week That Was*
    c. *Walter and Emily*
    d. *South of Sunset*

21. THE DOG
Initial Airdate: October 9, 1991

While by no means a complete dog, this unusually shaggy yarn drags a bit as Jerry becomes the doggedly miserable host to a highly annoying canine when its owner—a drunken fellow airline passenger named Gavin Palone, in a very inside showbiz reference to a prominent agent—apparently takes ill. Interestingly, someone named Tom Williams is credited for his Emmy-worthy performance as the Bark of the Dog in "The Dog."

22. THE LIBRARY
Initial Airdate: October 16, 1991

Check this one out: "The Library"—directed by Joshua White—is even more side-busting fun than the Dewey decimal system. When Jerry's busted by Bookman the library cop (Philip Baker Hall), we discover that our hero has failed to return a book that he took out back in 1971, though Jerry's not at fault here. In a related subplot that goes back to schooldays, George worries that a homeless man is on the streets because of him.

What's the title of the book Jerry has failed to return in "The Library"?

    a. *How to Win Friends and Influence People*
    b. *The First Book of Shtick*
    c. *Are You There, God? It's Me, Newman*
    d. *Tropic of Cancer*

23. THE PARKING GARAGE
Initial Airdate: October 30, 1991

Some *Seinfeld* fans could happily stay stuck in "The Parking Garage" forever, while others like myself react poorly to this intentionally claustrophobic episode in which the gang gets stuck in a Garden State mall parking area. Considering Jerry Seinfeld's reported past brush with Scientology, there is also a very interesting little scene in which George manages to offend a Scientology follower with a casual comment.

Which of the following actors is not *a reported Scientologist?*
  a. Kirstie Alley
  b. Tom Cruise
  c. Albert Brooks
  d. John Travolta

24. THE CAFE
Initial Airdate: November 6, 1991

Seinfeld always offers its viewers a little food for thought, and that's just what's on the menu in this mildly tasty look at the dangers of the food trade, written by Tom Leopold. "Bad man" Jerry tries to help Babu (Brian George), a struggling Pakistani restaurateur in his neighborhood, and ends up only making matters much worse for him. Elaine takes an IQ test for cheating George—who is trying to impress gal pal Monica (Dawn Arnemann)—with far from MENSA-ish results.

What would George have had to score on his IQ test to get into MENSA?
  a. 69
  b. 100
  c. 132
  d. 164

25. THE TAPE
Initial Airdate: November 13, 1991

A hairy and hilarious episode, this tale of "The Tape" finds the follicly challenged George understandably frustrated with the bald life. In a less receding subplot, Elaine secretly talks dirty into Jerry's tape recorder, in the process turning on everyone including lusty baldy George. Directed, like "The Truth," by David Steinberg rather than the usual Tom Cherones.

While George may have a problem with the bald thing, gorgeously coiffed Elaine never has. Which one of these hair care products does Julia Louis-Dreyfus endorse?
  a. Paul Masson chocolate hair mousse
  b. Pure Elements
  c. Clairol Nice & Easy
  d. Pendant Haircare Products

26. THE NOSE JOB
Initial Airdate: November 20, 1991

A deeply funny and deeply shallow episode written by Peter Mehlman, "The Nose Job" features Jerry debating whether or not to date Isabel, an otherwise uninteresting beauty, for the obvious and highly visible reasons. On the flip side of this issue, George attempts to manipulate his new interest, Audrey, into going under the knife for a little bit of the title cosmetic surgery.

Tawny Kitaen—who appears as Jerry's attractive love interest in "The Nose Job"—appeared in a video for which of the following bands?
   a. Whitesnake
   b. Toto
   c. Poison
   d. The Kingston Trio

27. THE STRANDED
Initial Airdate: November 27, 1991

Apparently, "The Stranded" was itself somewhat of a stranded show for a period—this episode was originally meant to air during the second season of *Seinfeld,* and in an unusual move Jerry Seinfeld introduced it as such when it finally aired for the first time. Party protocol and its eventual fallout are wonderfully examined here. The jerky party host ends up bringing a hooker to apartment 5A, and George screws up with another interoffice love connection.

"The Stranded" features actor Michael Chiklis as the pandering party host who briefly turns Jerry's pad into a house of ill repute. What TV series turned Chiklis into an unlikely, Costanza-like sex symbol?
   a. *Suddenly Chiklis*
   b. *JAG*
   c. *The Commish*
   d. *The Single Hairless Guy*

28. THE ALTERNATE SIDE
Initial Airdate: December 4, 1991

When naysayers worried early on about *Seinfeld* possibly being "too New York" for its own good, they might have been thinking of episodes like "The Alternate Side," which partly hinges on some familiarity with the twenty-four-hour parking holocaust that is Manhattan. Talking about Manhattan, master thespian Kramer gets a walk-on in a Woody Allen movie here, while Elaine dates a gentleman of a certain age.

Which Seinfeld star has really acted with Woody Allen?
   a. Jerry Seinfeld
   b. Wayne Knight
   c. Julia Louis-Dreyfus
   d. George Steinbrenner

SEINING OFF
NORM MACDONALD on *Seinfeld*

One of America's wisest wise-asses, Norm MacDonald is perhaps best known for having delivered the "fake news" on **Saturday Night Live's** *Weekend Update as well as serving for years as the show's all-around Dr. Sardonicus.*

The thing about *Seinfeld* that I would say is that they shouldn't feel bad, you know. I hear all the critics and I watch the show and I do not think it's about nothing. So I don't think they should feel bad. It's about something.

29. THE RED DOT
Initial Airdate: December 11, 1991

Bargain shopping has rarely proven as much fun as it gets to be in "The Red Dot," Michael J. Fox's favorite episode (see page 3), which finds the notoriously tight-with-a-buck George buying Elaine a sweater that's been discounted due to the title flaw and then passing it off to the cleaning lady with whom he has just had sex. Also in this Larry David beauty, Jerry ends up bringing about the sobriety downfall of Elaine's alcoholic love interest.

Which of the following movies starred David Naughton, who plays Elaine's recovering alcoholic boyfriend, Dick, in "The Red Dot"?
    a. *An American Werewolf in London*
    b. *Teen Wolf*
    c. *The Postman*
    d. *Citizen Kane*

30. THE SUBWAY
Initial Airdate: January 8, 1992

Seinfeld has always offered lots of moving, underground comedy and this excellent Larry Charles–penned episode is no exception. Among numerous other accomplishments, "The Subway"—in which the gang encounters some significant transportation problems—is an impressive technical achievement, considering that this altogether convincing subterranean comedy was shot on a Studio City soundstage with only one half of a train and a lot of fancy, inventive camera work. A lasting erotic image: George's bad brush with kinky handcuffing.

At which of the following famed New York restaurants does Jerry end up dining with the naked man he meets in "The Subway"?
  a. The Stork Club
  b. The Carnegie Deli
  c. Nathan's
  d. Tavern on the Green

31. THE PEZ DISPENSER
Initial Airdate: January 15, 1992

A snappy and delicious little comic confection written by Larry David, "The Pez Dispenser" features *Seinfeld*'s first exploration of the key concept of "the hand" when George—always one to plan ahead—attempts to gain the upper hand in a relationship by making a preemptive breakup. The fearless Kramer becomes a member of the Polar Bear Club, and Jerry uses the title prop to comic effect.

32. THE SUICIDE
Initial Airdate: January 29, 1992

Suicide is more than painless here in this episode written by Tom Leopold, it's pretty hilarious too. In "The Suicide," Jerry benefits from the attempted suicide of neighbor Martin when his sexy girlfriend, Gina, starts hitting on Jerry. A Drake's coffee cake figures in the episode, but that's by no means the only high-calorie addition to *Seinfeld* here—this was also the first episode to let us see Newman in all his glory. Fun *Seinfeld* family fact revealed in "The Suicide": George mentions having a brother.

On which of the following NBC series has Wayne Knight also made frequent appearances?
  a. *Just Shoot Me*
  b. *3rd Rock from the Sun*
  c. *Suddenly Susan*
  d. *Men Behaving Badly*

33. THE FIX-UP
Initial Airdate: February 5, 1992

Larry Charles and Elaine Pope won an Emmy for Outstanding Writing in a Comedy Series—and deservedly so—for this excellent episode in which, after some moderately heated debate, Elaine and Jerry fix up George with the whiny but lovable Cynthia, who has low dating standards. Things progress surprisingly quickly and by half hour's end, George has been confronted by the very real possibility that there could soon be another Costanza walking uncomfortably among us.

Maggie Jakobson—a.k.a. Maggie Jakobson Wheeler—who plays the desperate, bulimic but lovable Cynthia in "The Fix-Up," is also familiar for a recurring role in which of the following sitcoms?

   a. *Friends*
   b. *Dweebs*
   c. *Cleghorne!*
   d. *Pauly*

34. THE BOYFRIEND
Initial Airdate: February 12, 1992

Written by Larry David and Larry Levin, "The Boyfriend" arguably remains the best hourlong *Seinfeld* episode, with some brilliant homoerotic overtones and fine underplaying. Jerry makes a new pal at the gym—baseball great Keith Hernandez—only to find he's losing Keith to Elaine. The JFK parody scenario here is dead-on brilliant. Also entirely unforgettable is George's pants-down fall from the bathroom in a mad rush for the phone in an attempt to keep his unemployment benefits coming.

Mets great Keith Hernandez won two world championship titles with which two teams?

   a. Mets and Indians
   b. Mets and Cardinals
   c. Cardinals and Yankees
   d. NY Liberty and Houston Comets

George does a decent Jose Jimenez imitation in "The Boyfriend." What comedian invented this once popular comedy character?

   a. Kenny Bania
   b. Bill Dana
   c. Flip Wilson
   d. Larry David

35. THE LIMO
Initial Airdate: February 26, 1992

The wacky side of that whole wild neo-Nazism craze is the surprising focus of "The Limo." In this unusually political episode written by Larry Charles and Marc Jaffe, Jerry and George's pursuit of a free ride from the airport leads to the pair ending up with some frightening young fascists who have somehow confused George with a noted but extremely secretive Aryan writer.

36. THE GOOD SAMARITAN
Initial Airdate: March 4, 1992

A hit-and-run episode in which Jerry tries to do the right thing about a car accident but then tries to score with a fetching but irresponsible motorist, played by Helen Slater. Kramer, meanwhile, has a psychotic reaction to the voice of famously leggy *Entertainment Tonight* hostess Mary Hart. Auteur alert:

"The Good Samaritan" was directed by *Seinfeld*'s own Jason Alexander—the only time to date that one of the stars of the series has been so credited.

Who of the following was not *a host of* Entertainment Tonight?
a. Dixie Whatley
b. Tim Whatley
c. Leeza Gibbons
d. John Tesh

Actress Helen Slater did not *appear in which of the following movies:*
a. *The Legend of Billie Jean*
b. *Supergirl*
c. *The Full Monty*
d. *Lassie*

37. THE LETTER
Initial Airdate: March 25, 1992

Love and copyright violation collide in this literate comedy of stolen letters, written by Larry David. In "The Letter," Jerry has a love interest named Nina (Catherine Keener) who doesn't credit her literary sources, while Kramer poses for a painting and finds some fancy new admirers. Elaine's stubbornness causes some big, unsportsmanlike Yankee Stadium trouble in this slightly plot heavy and not quite "Letter" perfect episode that doesn't rank with David's best.

38. THE PARKING SPACE
Initial Airdate: April 22, 1992

A gang get-together for a boxing match on television turns into a fight of a different sort on the all-too-traveled streets of Manhattan. Beloved by many *Seinfeld* fans, this episode proved to be a believable but not particularly riveting one that deals with such enduring Big Apple issues as parallel parking—which (surprise, surprise) turns out to be George's forte—and the enduring dearth of really good spaces on the street. Along the way, we also learn that the Costanzas as a people simply refuse to pay for it—parking, that is.

What recent hit series was cocreated by Greg Daniels, who cowrote "The Parking Space" with Larry David?
a. *King of the Hill*
b. *Spin City*
c. *Touched by an Angel*
d. *Dr. Quinn, Medicine Woman*

Topic for further discussion: Why the hell do these hard-core Manhattanites end up driving so much?

39. THE KEYS
Initial Airdate: May 6, 1992

In the strong Larry Charles–penned "The Keys," the largely one-way apartment key exchange between Jerry and Kramer goes bad, and Kramer for some reason takes this as his cue to finally exit New York and head to Hollywood. For a frightening few moments here, it actually appears as though our *Seinfeld* fab four may be reduced to a power trio.

Which of the following actresses makes a cameo appearance as herself during Kramer's trip to Tinseltown in "The Keys"?
   a. Butterfly McQueen
   b. Gloria Stuart
   c. Pam Grier
   d. Candice Bergen

THE FOURTH SEASON

40. THE TRIP, PART I

Initial Airdate: August 12, 1992

Westward ho-ho, as *Seinfeld* takes an amusing bicoastal turn when George accompanies Jerry to Los Angeles for a *Tonight Show* stand-up spot in this season opener. While there, George manages in short order to piss off assorted celebs George Wendt, Fred Savage and Corbin Bernsen. In scenes that are fantastically cringe worthy, Jerry bombs on the show and Kramer gets mistaken for a celebrated local serial killer.

What's the name of Fred Savage's new TV series?
   a. *Working Again*
   b. *Working*
   c. *The Working Years*
   d. *Growing Pains: The Later Years*

True or false: Before L.A. Law, *Corbin Bernson* was actually a top stand-up comedian who earned more money per show than Jerry Seinfeld did at his peak.

41. THE TRIP, PART II

Initial Airdate: August 19, 1992

Like Woody Allen in the memorable Los Angeles scenes from *Annie Hall*, the *Seinfeld* gang are hilariously out of place in "The Trip, Part II," as Jerry and George make their way around El Lay and try to help wanted man Kramer, eventually running into the real serial killer, called the "Smog Strangler." By show's end, the K man is thankfully once again back in the Big Apple bosom and across the hall where he belongs.

Which of the following actors from a notable show business family plays the real "Smog Strangler" in "The Trip, Part II"?
   a. Daniel Baldwin
   b. Jim Belushi
   c. Clint Howard
   d. David Arquette

42. THE PITCH/THE TICKET

Initial Airdate: September 16, 1992

This one-hour doubleheader, written by Larry David—now split into two shows for syndication—offers a wonderfully self-referential, even cannibalistic look at TV, with George and Jerry's inspired notion of a show "about nothing" (as history will prove, truly a groundbreaking idea!). Providing comic fodder for three seasons, George and Susan Biddle Ross (Heidi Swedberg) begin their courtship.

43. THE WALLET

Initial Airdate: September 23, 1992

In from the Sunshine State, Jerry's father Morty is outraged by what he believes to be an act of larceny at the office of a prominent medical specialist, in a hilarious, over-the-top performance by actor Barney Martin. George tries with little success to do big business with NBC, and Elaine is still attempting to shake off her love-struck, unbalanced shrink, Dr. Reston, played with Freudian glee by Stephen McHattie.

Where can we assume George and Jerry's meetings with NBC take place?

    a. 129 West 81st Street, New York

    b. World Trade Center, New York

    c. Burbank, California

    d. 30 Rockefeller Plaza, New York

44. THE WATCH

Initial Airdate: September 30, 1992

That damned watch—thrown away by Jerry back in "The Pitch"—is just one of the items on the menu of topics discussed when Jerry dines with his parents and the always appetizing Uncle Leo in a meal begun in "The Wallet." Ace negotiator George irks NBC's Dalrymple (Bob Balaban, who seems born to play NBC president Warren Littlefield). *Seinfeld*'s so sharp it can even make a network seem funny.

45. THE BUBBLE BOY

Initial Airdate: October 7, 1992

The Boy in the Plastic Bubble was never like this fantastically prickly episode. A sharp and rather edgy piece of work, "The Bubble Boy" finds Jerry guilt-tripped by a loving father (onetime *Saturday Night Live* cast member Brian Doyle Murray) into visiting his sick son, a Jerry fan. The kid turns out to be a real jerk—albeit a hermetically sealed jerk—

who eventually comes to blows with George. And sometimes a cigar is not just a cigar—in "The Bubble Boy," Kramer destroys a cabin with a Cuban.

Which actor was the original 1970s "Boy in the Bubble"?
  a. Robby Benson
  b. John Travolta
  c. Paul Simon
  d. Michael Jackson

Who is Brian Doyle Murray's sibling?
  a. Murray the K
  b. Anne Murray
  c. Murray the Cab Driver
  d. Bill Murray

46. THE CHEEVER LETTERS
Initial Airdate: October 28, 1992

Few sitcoms would make comic hay of the sexual predilection of a late great American literary figure. Thus, "The Cheever Letters" must be considered an especially distinguished episode of *Seinfeld*. The highlight here comes when the horror of the writing process is laid bare in a painfully funny sequence as Jerry and George attempt with woefully little success to get a start on their pilot script for *The Seinfeld Project*. In another sign of more potential in-law mishagas to come, George has some rather serious trouble bonding with Susan's tense, tony

folks, played by Grace Zabriskie and Warren Frost.

What other TV series did Grace Zabriskie and Warren Frost appear in together?
  a. *The Benny Hill Show*
  b. *Nothing Sacred*
  c. *Twin Peaks*
  d. *Still the Beaver*

47. THE OPERA
Initial Airdate: November 4, 1992

"The Opera" is as much fun as three—or possibly even four—tenors. Elaine is the object of insane desire in this Larry Charles–written episode, in which she splits up with Crazy Joe Davola when the wack job demonstrates why his nickname is "Crazy." Even non–opera buffs will want to catch the sight of Kramer and George—who's wearing a torturously tight tuxedo—scalping opera tickets.

What well-known opera does the gang attend a performance of during "The Opera"?
  a. *Tommy*
  b. *The Barber of Park Slope*
  c. *Madame Iron Butterfly*
  d. *I Pagliacci*

48. THE VIRGIN

Initial Airdate: November 11, 1992

Being totally chaste has rarely been as much lusty fun as it is in "The Virgin," which was written by Peter Mehlman with Peter and Bob Farrelly, later of *Dumb & Dumber* fame. As the cute closet consultant and title woman of remarkable restraint, actress Jane Leeves is a pure—for Jerry, too pure—delight. George decides he should drop Susan so that he can upgrade to an even better significant other when he becomes a TV big shot. A Must-See TV note: After the first run of "The Virgin," Kramer—and thus Michael Richards—turned up on an episode of *Mad About You.*

Jane Leeves currently stars in a TV series that features a cute pooch. What is the name of this show?
   a. *Mad About You*
   b. *Frasier*
   c. *Dr. Quinn, Medicine Woman*
   d. *Ellen*

Like Michael Richards, what other NBC Must-See TV babe has done double duty on her show and Mad About You*?*
   a. Brooke Shields
   b. Murray the dog
   c. Lisa Kudrow
   d. Courteney Cox

49. THE CONTEST

Initial Airdate: November 18, 1992

As Larry David once told *Laugh Factory* magazine, "You write about what you know." Well, David won a richly deserved Emmy for this total masturbatory masterpiece. After Mrs. Costanza catches George abusing himself, the gang bets—$100 for the gentlemen, $150 for the lady—to see who can remain master of their domain for the longest time. By engaging in a delicate ballet of double-talk, *Seinfeld* manages to make masturbation funnier than Philip Roth ever did. All this, sponge baths, a virgin and JFK Jr. too make this that rare "Contest" in which everybody wins.

"The Contest" was the first episode to feature Estelle Harris as George's mother, Estelle Costanza. What was the name of the woeful sitcom starring Shelley Long and Treat Williams in which Harris appeared?
   a. *Cheerless*
   b. *Jewish American Prince of the City*
   c. *Dweebs*
   d. *Good Advice*

50. THE AIRPORT

Initial Airdate: November 25, 1992

Class consciousness strikes the world of *Seinfeld* to brilliant effect in the high-flying "The Airport"—one of Larry Charles's true flights of genius. After their flight gets canceled, Jerry and Elaine play out an utterly inspired look at the disparate joys and pains of the in-flight caste system as they fight over who will get a first-class seat, while George and Kramer get in trouble down on the ground.

51. THE PICK

Initial Airdate: December 16, 1992

An especially excellent comedy of errors written by Larry David and Marc Jaffe, "The Pick" deals with some important issues you probably won't find on your average sitcom—the risks of public nose picking and the devastating social impact of accidental nipple display on a seasonal greeting card. All this and the unforgettable sight of Kramer—he of the distinguished buttocks—as an underwear model make this a very solid "Pick." Unresolved family moment: Elaine gets a call from her sister Gail.

52. THE MOVIE

Initial Airdate: January 6, 1993

Hot on the heels of "The Pick" comes yet another comedy of errors, but sadly, this episode comes off as a small error in its own right. "The Movie" is like an all-too-disappointing little-screen sequel to the more spicy "The Chinese Restaurant," only this time around the gang has every sort of difficulty just trying to meet and go to a movie together on a night when Jerry has double-booked himself in the clubs.

In "The Movie," what's the name of the fast-food joint whose hot dogs obsess Kramer to distraction?
  a. Dogs "R" Us
  b. The Dog Soldiers
  c. A Real Porker
  d. Papaya King

53. THE VISA

Initial Airdate: January 27, 1993

No doubt there have been times—though probably very, very few—when Jerry Seinfeld's tried to be funny and wasn't. The comedic high point of "The Visa," however, is Jerry trying quite hard *not* to be funny, and failing to do so. At George's request, Jerry tries his somber best not to upstage George in front of his new lawyer girlfriend, Cheryl (Maggie Han). Kramer gets booted from baseball fantasy camp for punching a baseball legend.

While Jerry tries hard not to be funny in "The Visa," he sure tries hard to be humorous in his commercials for which credit card company?
  a. Visa
  b. MasterCard
  c. Discover
  d. American Express

54. THE SHOES
Initial Airdate: February 4, 1993

While one feels like a heel for saying so, *Seinfeld* doesn't put its best foot forward in "The Shoes." Dalrymple spends much of the episode in the bathroom, and while you won't be retching, there are fewer laughs than usual. Let me get this off of my chest now: This episode's mostly a breast-obsessed bore in which George and Jerry try to keep their NBC series a reality despite some professionally suicidal lust that George expresses for the big boss's daughter Molly. Jerry runs into an old gal pal, Gail (Anita Barone), who ends up pissing off Elaine and kissing Kramer. Elaine's whole shoe subplot is one big mediocre misfit.

55. THE OUTING
Initial Airdate: February 11, 1993

Get this straight: "The Outing," written by Larry Charles—the near perfect episode that launched the useful catch phrase, "Not that there's anything wrong with that"—has virtually nothing wrong with it at all. In "The Outing," a student reporter somehow gets the wrong idea about the close nature of Jerry and companion George's relationship. Of course, the fact remains that these two do make one hell of a cute couple, and this remains one hell of an out-and-out brilliant episode.

Who plays Sharon—the comely cub reporter who falsely comes to believe that Jerry and George are a romantic couple—in "The Outing"?
  a. Ellen DeGeneres
  b. Carl Bernstein
  c. Paula Marshall
  d. Monica Lewinsky

56. THE OLD MAN
Initial Airdate: February 18, 1993

Having dealt with the delicate matter of sexual preference so effectively in the previous episode, *Seinfeld* turns its comic attentions to age discrimination and charity in a fairly uproarious and head-on manner in "The Old Man" as Jerry,

George and Elaine all volunteer to work with the elderly in order to add a little meaning to their less-than-full lives. Predictably, perhaps, things do not go well or particularly heartwarmingly for pretty much anyone involved.

In "The Old Man," Jason Alexander can be seen wearing a shirt with the title of which Broadway show that he once starred in?
   a. *Broadway Bound*
   b. *Bent*
   c. *Rent*
   d. *Hair*

57. THE IMPLANT
Initial Airdate: February 25, 1993

Only three episodes after the breast-obsessed episode "The Shoes" comes this far stronger show. In "The Implant" Jerry is obsessed with whether his statuesque new love interest, Sidra, has had a little surgical help upstairs; Elaine does a little detective work for him at the gym and finds out the truth. Also on the comic hit list: Kramer believes he's spotted author Salman Rushdie at the gym.

Which of the following well-known actresses appears in the supporting role of Sidra, the suitably stacked object of Jerry's horny curiosity in "The Implant"?
   a. Mariel Hemingway
   b. Dolly Parton
   c. Teri Hatcher
   d. Jayne Mansfield

58. THE JUNIOR MINT
Initial Airdate: March 18, 1993

Before it became blown up into a big legal matter, "The Junior Mint" was simply a typically outstanding and refreshing episode written by Andy Robin. The verdict is in: This is not only a winning episode, it also made for some riveting *Seinfeld*-related viewing on Court TV. Famously, Jerry forgets the name of the woman he's dating, though he recalls that it rhymes with a certain part of the female anatomy. Elaine is typically shallow with a former beau. As for the title, a Junior Mint ends up somewhere that it shouldn't.

What's the name of the actress who plays the girlfriend whose name Jerry finds he can't recall in "The Junior Mint"?
   a. Delores O'Rioden
   b. Mulva Streep
   c. Susan Walters
   d. Kitty O'Shea

MEDICAL NOTE

On October 28, 1997, the *New York Times* reported the identification of a brand-new medical condition—the *Seinfeld* syndrome. Dr. Stephen V. Cox and two of his colleagues from Lahey Hitchcock Medical Center in Burlington, Massachusetts, wrote a letter in the journal *Catheterization and Cardiovascular Diagnosis* about their treatment of a sixty-two-year-old gentleman who fainted "at least three times" while watching *Seinfeld.* Apparently and understandably, he laughed so hard at George Costanza's behavior that he lost consciousness.

Thankfully, the doctors were able to treat him, but still we feel his pain.

59. THE SMELLY CAR

Initial Airdate: April 15, 1993

Fortunately Smell-O-Vision was not used in the production of this pungent episode which bravely confronts the oft-overlooked issue of bad body odor getting transferred by valet parkers. The haughty restaurateur here is played by former movie star and onetime Power Station singer Michael Des Barres. George runs into Susan and an intriguing new love interest at the video store.

Which of the following movies did Michael Des Barres star in?
  a. *Arachnophobia*
  b. *To Sir with Love*
  c. *Good Will Hunting*
  d. *My Mother the Car: The Film*

60. THE HANDICAP SPOT

Initial Airdate: May 13, 1993

One of *Seinfeld*'s special parking-related episodes that always hits the "Spot." While buying an engagement gift for the Drake, George incites an angry mob by parking in a handicapped space at the mall. Kramer falls hard for a wheelchair-bound woman victimized by the mishap. This Larry David–penned episode originally featured John Randolph as Frank Costanza, though Jerry Stiller later replaced him in scenes shot for syndicated showings of "The Handicap Spot." Sadly, the Drake and the Drakette split.

Sure, we've all gotta love the Drake, but can you pick which of the following well-known stand-up comedians played the Drake in "The Handicap Spot"?
  a. Carrot Top
  b. Robert Klein
  c. Rick Overton
  d. Jimmie "J.J." Walker

61. THE PILOT

Initial Airdate: May 20, 1993

Rarely has TV taken such a long, hard, mocking look at itself as *Seinfeld* does in "The Pilot," a one-hour season closer written by Larry David in which we watch Jerry and George go through the process of mounting their show-about-nothing-within-a-show-about-nothing pilot. It's amusing to watch the casting process as a bizarro counter-reality of how *Seinfeld* could have gone wrong early on. Especially funny is contentious, raisin-stealing TV Kramer Tom Peppers, played by Larry Hankin.

Larry Hankin has appeared on which other NBC show, as a character named Mr. Heddes?
 a. *3rd Rock from the Sun*
 b. *Friends*
 c. *Veronica's Closet*
 d. *Union Square*

THE FIFTH SEASON

62. THE MANGO

Initial Airdate: September 16, 1993

Another tactfully filthy *Seinfeld* in which we share George's sexual suffering and angst when he gets "the tap" from Karen (Lisa Edelstein) while pleasuring her. Meanwhile, Elaine lets Jerry in on an unsettling sexual secret that drives them into bed together. The title of "The Mango" refers to a fairly ripe subplot in which Kramer gets banned from his beloved fruit stand.

Lisa Edelstein—who plays Karen, the woman who gets more satisfaction from risotto than from George in "The Mango"—starred in which of the following series?
   a. *When Harry Met Sally: The Series*
   b. *Relativity*
   c. *Party Girl*
   d. *Meego*

Topic for further discussion: Why do you think Larry David—who cowrote "The Mango" with Lawrence H. Levy—originally credited himself as Buck Dancer?

63. THE PUFFY SHIRT

Initial Airdate: September 23, 1993

"The Puffy Shirt," written by Larry David, features *Seinfeld*'s finest fashion faux pas and loads of laughs as we get to see Jerry squirm miserably in what may be the ugliest shirt to appear on a sitcom. The motto here is to speak softly and carry a puffy shirt, when Jerry agrees, after a conversation with a too-quiet friend of Kramer's, to wear a godawful piratelike blouse on an important upcoming TV spot. All this and the great Jerry Stiller's official debut as Frank Costanza. By the way, did anyone else notice how closely Jerry resembles eighties Brit rocker Adam Ant while wearing that pirate puffy shirt?

Jerry Stiller is married to which famous comedian?
   a. Phyllis Diller
   b. Anne Meara
   c. Janeane Garofalo
   d. Joan Rivers

Rough Crowd: Crazy Joe Davola reacts rather poorly to what he sees in "The Pilot."

On which of the following TV shows does Jerry accidentally agree to wear the puffy shirt?

    a. *The Sean "Puffy" Combs Family Hour*

    b. *The Rosie O'Donnell Show*

    c. *Today*

    d. *Regis and Kathie Lee*

64. THE GLASSES

Initial Airdate: September 30, 1993

Sure, *Seinfeld* is almost always a sight for sore eyes, but it can be a tad hard to see why at times in the slightly strained "The Glasses," which sadly is simply not one of *Seinfeld*'s more visionary episodes. Dog bites Elaine in this warm-weather episode, and Jerry goes blind with jealousy when the ocularly challenged George mistakenly believes he has spotted Jerry's gal pal Amy kissing his ever-so-elusive cousin Jeffrey, when in truth it's a woman making out with a horse of another color.

65. THE SNIFFING ACCOUNTANT

Initial Airdate: October 7, 1993

White line fever strikes *Seinfeld* in this not-remotely-taxing episode written by David and Seinfeld, that's even more fun than an extended IRS audit. In "The Sniffing Accountant," Jerry becomes extremely concerned when he surmises that the sniff-ing of his accountant Barry Profit may be the result of a drug problem that could land him and some of the other *Seinfeld* gang in grave fiscal danger. Meanwhile, despite the considerable support of father Frank, George's flirtatiousness gets him in and out of the bra game in short order.

John Kapelos—who guests as Jerry's accountant Barry Profit—was in the cast of which of the following justifiably obscure nineties television series?

    a. *Forever Knight*

    b. *Mr. Rhodes*

    c. *Good Behavior*

    d. *Presidential Knee Pads*

66. THE BRIS

Initial Airdate: October 14, 1993

With the typically sharp "The Bris," *Seinfeld* proves once again why the show has been able to stay on the cutting edge of comedy. A possible alternative title for this odd episode might be "Of Circumcisions and Pig Men" or "The Nutty *Mohel*." New godparents Elaine and Jerry sweat out their bris duties, while Kramer believes he's spotted a horrible product of genetic engineering—a "pig man," he claims—while at the hospital. Leave it to *Seinfeld* to match Judaism and a pork-related subplot in a single episode.

67. THE LIP READER

Initial Airdate: October 28, 1993

Tennis and faked handicaps, anyone? It's a love match in "The Lip Reader," written by future *Alright, Already* star Carol Leifer, when Jerry falls for Laura, a deaf B.L.—or Beautiful Lineswoman—at the U.S. Open tennis tournament. Elaine feigns deafness to avoid a conversation, and George's latest flame, Gwen, breaks up with him because of a very public display of sloppy eating. Great moment in *Seinfeld* sports: Kramer as the world's oldest ball man crashing into Monica Seles. *Seinfeld* serves up another ace here.

Which of the following Oscar-winning actresses plays Laura, the U.S. Open tennis lineswoman who confuses six *for* sex *in "The Lip Reader"?*
   a. Olympia Dukakis
   b. Kathy Bates
   c. Marlee Matlin
   d. Marisa Tomei

68. THE NON-FAT YOGURT

Initial Airdate: November 4, 1993

An unusually weighty and obscenity-laced episode, "The Non-Fat Yogurt" features a fact-finding mission to discover just how non-fat the yogurt really is at the new dessert spot in which Kramer's invested. Jerry—not a comedian known for working "blue"—influences an impressionable child for the worse with his cursing. A not-so-brilliant idea from Elaine provokes a NYC political firebomb.

Which of the following real-life New York City political figures makes a cholesterol-related cameo appearance in "The Non-Fat Yogurt"?
   a. Mayor David Dinkins
   b. Mayor Edward Koch
   c. Mayor Fiorello La Guardia
   d. Mayor Rudy Giuliani

69. THE BARBER

Initial Airdate: November 11, 1993

For hard-core Georgeophiles like myself, "The Barber" will forever be unofficially dubbed "The Pensky File," since far and away the most cutting element of the episode is George's unique take on how to get ahead in business without really working. Alexander is at the height of his powers here, as our demented Dilbert—never being one to stand on ceremony, formality or logic—simply starts going to work at a "small and prestigious" rest stop–supply company before he has ever actually been hired.

Fruit of a Loon: Kramer endures food issues in "The Mango."

70. THE MASSEUSE
Initial Airdate: November 18, 1993

Hands-on humor marks "The Masseuse," written by Peter Mehlman, in which Jerry grows increasingly tense and aggravated by his strange inability to get his new masseuse girlfriend, Jody (Jennifer Coolidge), to give him a sample of her touchy professional services, while Jody won't even talk to George. As for Elaine, she tries to get her boyfriend (Anthony Cistaro) to change his mood-killing name because it causes her considerable embarrassment. A touching celebration of the depth of Elaine's shallowness.

In "The Masseuse" Elaine dates a man who shares the same name with which of the following prominent individuals?
  a. President Abraham Lincoln
  b. Rock star Meat Loaf
  c. Pope John Paul II
  d. Serial killer Joel Rifkin

71. THE CIGAR STORE INDIAN
Initial Airdate: December 9, 1993

In "The Cigar Store Indian"—a standout episode written by Tom Gammill and Max Pross—political correctness rears its ugly, humor-challenged wooden head when Jerry inadvertently offends his Native American love interest by purchasing an inappropriate, un-PC gift. On the subway, Elaine meets a total geek with a passion for her own considerable charms and for a certain popular TV periodical. And in a tremendously credible cameo, news personality Al Roker is seen stealing a gyro sandwich.

Al Roker shares the same network as Jerry and George do for their short-lived show. What show has made Roker a beloved national star?
  a. *Seaquest DSV*
  b. *Dateline*
  c. *Today*
  d. *When Weathermen Attack*

72. THE CONVERSION
Initial Airdate: December 16, 1993

It's a funny matter of faux faith and fantasized fungi in "The Conversion," a Bruce Kirschbaum–penned episode, which finds the ever-shallow Brother George deciding to convert to a new religion in a hilariously desperate and ineffectual bid to hold on to a new girlfriend. Judgmental Jerry goes bonkers with suspicion when his new love interest's medicine cabinet becomes a Pandora's box of paranoia. Kramer's ample animal magnetism creates a temporary spiritual crisis for a love-struck novice, played by Molly Hagen. It's episodes like this wholly entertaining one that have helped make *Seinfeld* tubular religion.

73. THE STALL
Initial Airdate: January 6, 1994

In addition to dealing with the always pressing matter of bathroom etiquette, "The Stall" offers a lesser variation on "The Boyfriend"—only instead of Keith Hernandez, this time it's George who is desperate to hang with Elaine's athletic new boy toy, whom Jerry correctly calls a "mimbo." The boys go rock-climbing, and George and Kramer even do a little pre-Jewel yodeling. Kramer's dirty phone habit gets him in trouble with Jerry.

What onetime MTV personality plays the ultra-manly Tony in "The Stall"?
  a. Pauly Shore
  b. Bill Bellamy
  c. Butt-head
  d. Dan Cortese

True or false: Jami Gertz—who plays Jerry's girlfriend in "The Stall"—played Muffy Tepperman in the eighties cult-hit sitcom Square Pegs.

74. THE DINNER PARTY
Initial Airdate: February 3, 1994

A shaky comedy of errors as the gang gets waylaid trying to go to a dinner party in chilly weather. It's an exercise in frustration, but not one of scripter Larry David's best moments. Like the gang in this half hour, this episode takes too long to get where it's going. Whatever the flaws of "The Dinner Party," the concept of "lesser bobka" elucidated herein remains a tasty conceit.

75. THE MARINE BIOLOGIST
Initial Airdate: February 10, 1994

A *Moby Dick*-size whale of a classic episode, the masterfully written "The Marine Biologist"—penned by Ron Hague and Charlie Rubin—boasts some of the most enduring lines in all of *Seinfeld* history. They are delivered by George: "The sea was angry that day, my friends. Like an old man trying to send back soup at a deli." In a soulful and hilarious nod to the soul great Edwin Starr, Jerry convinces a shockingly gullible Elaine that the original title for *War and Peace* was *War—What Is It Good For?* Funnier than Tolstoy.

Winterwear of Their Discontent: The gang all bundled up in the seasonal "The Dinner Party."

Which of the following Taxi *figures makes a cameo in "The Marine Biologist"?*

    a. Carol Kane
    b. Jeff Conaway
    c. Marilu Henner
    d. Andy Kaufman

76. THE PIE

Initial Airdate: February 17, 1994

Ricky, the *TV-Guide*-and-Elaine-loving nerd who made such a striking impression in "The Cigar Store Indian," returns, as we discover in "The Pie" that he's designed a mannequin that looks quite a bit like *Seinfeld*'s fairest character of all. Neat freak Jerry has hygiene-related issues with another girlfriend, Audrey, and her chef father Poppie (the great Reni Santoni), who owns a restaurant. "The Pie" is mildly tasty.

77. THE STAND-IN
Initial Airdate: February 24, 1994

Jeez, talk about a tough crowd. Jerry nearly makes himself sick in "The Stand-In" trying to get a laugh out of his ailing friend, Fulton, who has been hospitalized and could be facing his last laugh. Elaine gets freaked out when she gets a little too much exposure from one of Jerry's softball pals, while Kramer—who gets a gig as a TV soap opera stand-in—encourages his little pal Mickey (Danny Woodburn) to wear lifts, a big move that backfires. Michael Richards and Woodburn have a strange, appealing chemistry not unlike Laurel and Hardy in hell.

78. THE WIFE
Initial Airdate: March 17, 1994

Jerry Seinfeld and wedding bells aren't a natural match. Marriage—even a fake marriage—is a *Seinfeld* rarity until "The Betrayed" in the ninth season. In "The Wife," Jerry's new girlfriend, Meryl, pretends to be his wife, for that most traditional and romantic of reasons—to

save on her dry-cleaning bill. Soon, of course, things go horribly wrong between the pseudo-spouses, as they also do when George thoughtlessly uses the health club shower in a pissy manner unbecoming a gentleman.

Which fetching Friends *star plays Jerry's make-believe spouse in "The Wife"?*
   a. Matt LeBlanc
   b. Jennifer Aniston
   c. Courteney Cox
   d. Marcel the Monkey

79. THE RAINCOATS
Initial Airdate: April 28, 1994

Personal space is at a premium in "The Raincoats," written by the David-Seinfeld and Gammill-Pross teams. Judge Reinhold earned an Emmy nomination—and a richly deserved one—for his memorable in-your-face guest spot as Aaron the Close Talker in the one-hour episode. There are parental tensions between the Seinfelds and Costanzas when the former come to town. Kramer and Morty decide to do some funny business in the raincoat trade. And with his folks staying in his apartment, Jerry gets caught sucking face with Rachel (Melanie Smith) at that most unlikely of make-out flicks, *Schindler's List.*

Dummy Act: Elaine meets her mirror-image mannequin in "The Pie."

80. THE FIRE

Initial Airdate: May 5, 1994

We've too rarely seen Jerry doing stand-up as part of the main action of an episode—"The Fire" is one exception. Here Kramer's annoying editor and girlfriend, Toby, heckles Jerry mercilessly from the audience on a night when he's being reviewed by *Entertainment Weekly*. Also, George panics when there's a fire during a kids' party at his new girlfriend's place. Jon Favreau—who would gain fame with *Swingers*—plays a real clown here. Still, "The Fire" never quite ignites.

Melanie Chartoff—who plays George's girlfriend in "The Fire"—was in the cast of ABC's early eighties comedy variety show Fridays. *Which of the following individuals was also in that cast?*
- a. Madeleine Albright
- b. Martin Lawrence
- c. Larry David
- d. Michael Dukakis

81. THE HAMPTONS
Initial Airdate: May 12, 1994

That most dreaded of male phenomena—I speak of course, friends, of post-swimming "shrinkage"—ruins a trip to the Hamptons. Jerry's weekend date—seen in "The Raincoats"—walks in on George, who is nude and in a diminished capacity after his dip in the ocean. By this time, George is already fuming, since everyone has seen his own date topless before he enjoyed that distinct pleasure himself, while the locals are in a frenzy over Kramer-related crimes, in this episode written by Peter Mehlman and Carol Leifer.

82. THE OPPOSITE
Initial Airdate: May 19, 1994

"The Opposite," from the pen of Andy Cowan, Larry David and Jerry Seinfeld, attracts almost anyone with a sense of humor. George turns his life around in a big way simply by doing the opposite of what he normally would do, while Elaine's fortunes take a dramatic turn for the worse after she makes an inappropriate candy stop. Among other attributes, "The Opposite" also introduces the show's unforgettable George Steinbrenner, voiced with great conviction by none other than Larry David. Extra credit for being hilarious even with a Kathie Lee Gifford and Regis Philbin cameo.

On which show has the real George Steinbrenner appeared?
- a. *Touched by a Yankee*
- b. *Saturday Night Live*
- c. *New York Undercover*
- d. *Spin City*

Kramer makes himself at home with Jerry and occasional business partner and gruff father figure Morty Seinfeld.

THE SIXTH SEASON

83. THE CHAPERONE
Initial Airdate: September 22, 1994

Hello, Mr. Pitt. Andy Ackerman took over direction of *Seinfeld* in this promising season opener, an early example of Ackerman's auteur-like genius in which we discover that the ever surprising Kramer has an incredible reservoir of inane beauty pageant knowledge when he comes to the aid of a contestant in her ultimately losing bid to become Miss America. At first, the Yankees cotton to George's idea for them to change their uniforms. Elaine—she of a certain vague Jackie O–like grace—finds herself changing jobs, from book editor to working with Mr. Pitt.

At which publishing company did Jacqueline Kennedy Onassis work as an editor?

    a. Random House
    b. Simon & Schuster
    c. Doubleday
    d. Pendant Publishing

84. THE BIG SALAD
Initial Airdate: September 29, 1994

Yes, Virginia, roughage can be a riot, and the proof is in the low-fat pudding in "The Big Salad," which was tossed by Larry David. Here a very big deal gets made about a small bill for a lite entrée. An especially petty Georgie Boy grows outraged by his girlfriend Julia when she gets the credit for his purchase of Elaine's leafy meal. Jerry makes a nauseating discovery about his love interest's romantic past—i.e., she dated Newman. Kramer gets involved in a very familiar and juicy crime story involving a prominent athlete. "The Big Salad" is one of those episodes that shows how *Seinfeld* has elevated pettiness to an art form.

85. THE PLEDGE DRIVE
Initial Airdate: October 6, 1994

Dan—the high-talking fellow whom Jerry upsets to no end in "The Pledge Drive"—is a fairly amusing character, though ultimately he's no match for such distinguished funny *Seinfeld* talkers as the close-talking Aaron in "The

Raincoats" or the low-talking Leslie of "The Puffy Shirt." Mr. Pitt starts an extremely unlikely Snickers-cutting craze, and the always civic-minded Jerry works a PBS fund-raising drive and causes his Nana to bounce some checks.

Which of the following actors plays Mr. Pitt in "The Pledge Drive" and other episodes?
  a. Brad Pitt
  b. Ian Abercrombie
  c. Ralph Macchio
  d. Anson Williams

86. THE CHINESE WOMAN
Initial Airdate: October 13, 1994

Any Ingmar Bergman–like peek inside the Costanzas' union is welcome, and in this delicious episode, the Costanzas' marriage is in trouble—*who knew?* The seemingly idyllic partnership of George's parents falls apart after Mr. Costanza is spotted in the city with a mysterious man in a cape (a searing if extremely abbreviated Larry David cameo). Kramer deals with sensitive infertility issues regarding his "boys" and Jerry meets up with his surprising-looking phone pal, whose name, Donna Chang, leads him to jump to some incorrect conclusions.

87. THE COUCH
Initial Airdate: October 27, 1994

Seinfeld may not have the ability to sell millions of books to the masses with a single plug *à la Oprah,* but that doesn't stop the show from getting bookish every once in a while. The highlight of this comfy "Couch" is the unforgettable and uproarious lengths George goes to so he can avoid reading the book his book group has selected. Less amusing, though politically interesting, is Elaine's split-up with Carl over her belief in a woman's right to choose in the matter of abortion.

Breakfast at Tiffany's, *the book George so strenuously tries to avoid in "The Couch," was written by whom?*
  a. Audrey Hepburn
  b. Truman Capote
  c. Norman Mailer
  d. Martha Stewart

88. THE GYMNAST
Initial Airdate: November 3, 1994

In "The Gymnast," George's unorthodox but curiously endearing bathroom habits score a perfect ten from this comedy judge as part of the very special *Seinfeld* Olympics. In this episode, written by Alec Berg and Jeff Schaeffer, Jerry dates Katya—the flexible Romanian title character—expecting that she will also have all the right moves during her performance in the sack. Kramer, meanwhile, suffers from kidney stones with slapstick grace.

89. THE SOUP

Initial Airdate: November 10, 1994

A season before "The Soup Nazi," soup is already the special of the day at *Seinfeld*. In this funny and flavorful "Soup," written by Fred Stoller, Jerry soon comes to regret taking a free suit from Kenny Bania (Stephen Hytner) because of his promise to buy the ever-annoying comedian a free meal in exchange for the designer threads. A nightmarish trip to Mendys leads to a lively debate about what exactly constitutes a meal. Elaine—the *Seinfeld* hostess with the mostest—has a visiting freeloader from across the Atlantic.

90. THE MOM & POP STORE

Initial Airdate: November 17, 1994

Name-dropping is an occasional *Seinfeld* sporting event, and in "The Mom & Pop Store," George name-drops with gusto, showing that he's so shallow and starstruck that he actually buys a used car because the salesman tells him that the auto was once owned by the great actor Jon Voight. Despite good intentions, Kramer has another bad brush

with capitalism in the form of a shoe repair store. Thanks to Elaine, Mr. Pitt gets to enjoy the Thanksgiving Day Parade—though it could be said that now that the show's in syndication, every day is really Thanksgiving Day for *Seinfeld*-heads.

Which company sponsors New York City's famous Thanksgiving Day Parade?
    a. Poppie's
    b. Papaya King
    c. Macy's
    d. Putumayo

In which movie did Jon Voight—who makes a cameo appearance in "The Mom & Pop Store"—not appear?
    a. *Anaconda*
    b. *Midnight Cowboy*
    c. *Urban Cowboy*
    d. *Heat*

91. THE SECRETARY

Initial Airdate: December 8, 1994

Jerry has serious dry-cleaning problems in this highly amusing episode written by Carol Leifer and the late Marjorie Gross, in which it becomes scandalously clear that Willie the dry cleaner (Joseph R. Sicari) and his wife, Donna (*Alright, Already*'s Mitzi McCall), are treating their customers' clothes like their own. As for the title, George rubs up a serious staffing problem despite hiring Ada, the initially plain firecracker of a secretary played by the always-funny Vicki Lewis. Kramer comes *this* close to hooking up with Uma Thurman. Auteur alert: "The Secretary" was directed not by Andy Ackerman, but David Owen Trainor.

In which of the following NBC shows does Vicki Lewis—who appears as George's surprisingly lusty secretary Ada in "The Secretary"—now star?
   a. *NewsRadio*
   b. *Law & Order*
   c. *ER*
   d. *Dateline NBC*

92. THE RACE
Initial Airdate: December 15, 1994
Think of "The Race" as *Chariots of Mire.* A *Seinfeld* grudge race is at the heart of this speedy episode in which Jerry re-runs a race with old schoolmate Duncan. And in an atypically political subplot where Karl and Groucho Marx come together to fine effect, Elaine gets blacklisted for Chinese food delivery because of the political affiliation of her new boyfriend, and Kramer becomes a very leftist—or should I say *Red*—department store Santa Claus.

93. THE SWITCH
Initial Airdate: January 5, 1995
Perhaps you have watched *Seinfeld* and thought that if only George and Jerry put their heads together and really tried to accomplish something useful for society, well, it might be a better world in which to live. Well, that's exactly what happens in this exemplary Bruce Kirschenbaum and Sam Kass–penned episode as the pair attempt to find their own holy grail—an answer to the age-old issue of how to pull off the nearly impossible roommate switch. George and Jerry acting like adolescent Einsteins in their dogged and doggish pursuit of this solution is one of the most moving male-bonding high points of the entire series. As if that weren't enough, Kramer's mom, Babs (Sheree North), pops up and Kramer's first name is finally revealed to the rest of the waiting world.

94. THE LABEL MAKER
Initial Airdate: January 19, 1995
Seinfeld is God's gift to TV that keeps on giving, and in "The Label Maker" the show deals with the societal ill of re-gifting—the timeless practice of passing along a gift found wanting to another innocent party. Label makers and Super Bowl tickets are passed around here, though few people end up

happy in the end. George, meanwhile, lives to regret his manipulation in getting his new girlfriend, Bonnie (Jessica Tuck), to dump her male roommate, whom he's wrongly perceived as some threat. Finally, though, the episode underwhelms because of the tiresome gamesmanship that gets out of hand between Kramer and Newman.

95. THE SCOFFLAW
Initial Airdate: January 26, 1995

Generally speaking, disease makes for successful, gripping TV, especially the dreaded movie-of-the-week variety. In "The Scofflaw," master thespian guest star Jon Lovitz offers a twist in which his character Gary the liar turns out to have been faking his cancer so that he can garner sympathy. The headstrong Elaine has a notably petty post-breakup battle of pride with her annoying ex-boyfriend Jake Jarmel, whom we first met in "The Opposite." Hair today, gone next epiode: George gets a scary hairpiece.

Which animated show prominently featured the voice of Jon Lovitz?
   a. *South Park*
   b. *Dr. Katz*
   c. *The Critic*
   d. *Capitol Critters*

96. THE BEARD
Initial Airdate: February 9, 1995

Not since the Great Roommate Switch of Episode 93 has a member of the *Seinfeld* gang dared to dream the impossible dream quite so boldly as in the Carol Leifer–written "The Beard," which finds Elaine attempting against all odds to bring an appealing man named Robert over to the heterosexual camp. Jerry takes a lie detector test to determine whether or not he watches a certain popular TV show despite his denial. A musical note: Robert, Elaine's object of desire, is played by Rob Mailhouse, who also plays with actor Keanu Reeves in the rock band Dogstar. This "Beard" will grow on people of all genders.

What TV show does Jerry secretly watch, as revealed by a lie detector test in "The Beard"?
   a. *The NewsHour with Jim Lehrer*
   b. *Melrose Place*
   c. *Masterpiece Theater*
   d. *The 700 Club*

97. THE KISS HELLO
Initial Airdate: February 16, 1995

"The Kiss Hello"—a Larry David–Jerry Seinfeld collaboration—pecks at such timely subjects as dated hair and forced interbuilding intimacy, as the gang discusses the retro hairstyle of Elaine's friend. Kramer's good-hearted attempt at apartment building *glasnost* eventually lands the less than touchy-feely Jerry in some hot water with the other residents.

In "The Kiss Hello," which of these sitcom stars plays Elaine's out-of-style pal Wendy?
a. Jennifer Aniston of *Friends*
b. Lea Thompson of *Caroline in the City*
c. Wendie Malick of *Just Shoot Me*
d. Lisa Whelchel of *The Facts of Life*

98. THE DOORMAN
Initial Airdate: February 23, 1995

Social theorists may long debate whether "The Doorman" is ultimately about class struggle or just the story of one particular working stiff in a uniform. Either way, really, the nasty and oddly resentful doorman at Mr. Pitt's apartment building lashes out here at Jerry in this episode written by Tom Gammill and Max Pross. Kramer also gets inventive in his effort to help Mr. Costanza's personal support problem with the revolutionary male bra known as the Bro, or alternatively the Manssier.

Which of the following veteran stand-up comedians plays the surly doorman with a huge chip on his proletariat shoulder in "The Doorman"?
a. Rip Taylor
b. Larry Miller
c. Emo Phillips
d. Jay Leno

99. THE JIMMY
Initial Airdate: March 16, 1995

In an age of pathological political correctness, *Seinfeld* is never afraid to loiter on that thin, rather well-traveled line between being offensive and hilarious. In "The Jimmy" Kramer reacts to the anesthesia of *Seinfeld* dentist Dr. Tim Whatley (Bryan Cranston) in such a way that he's mistaken for a mentally challenged person. Kramer is priceless here in his scene with music great Mel Tormé. Meanwhile, Jerry has his own dental dilemma. Third person–talking Jimmy (Anthony Starke) thinks that Jimmy might like to spend a little time with Elaine.

True or false: Mel Tormé, who sings for Kramer in "The Jimmy," once sang a song with the willfully weird band Was Not Was.

Kramer gets lost in
the Velvet Fog.

Evolution takes a holiday in "The Face Painter."

100. THE DOODLE
Initial Airdate: April 6, 1995

Perhaps it is only fitting that it's a Chunky candy wrapper that gives Newman away in "The Doodle," an episode far more forgettable than most, though it's the show's one hundredth episode. He is the guilty party and the cause of a series of escalating problems for Jerry, who must get his apartment fumigated when his parents are in town. And surprise, surprise, Jerry loses another girlfriend because of a hygiene-related issue. George finds a new girlfriend's less-than-flattering doodle of him worrying.

101. THE FUSILLI JERRY
Initial Airdate: April 27, 1995

High in both starch and laughs, "The Fusilli Jerry" finds artist Kramer showing off his pasta sculpture of his good friend and neighbor. Funnier still is the Kama Sutra according to *Seinfeld* subplot in which Jerry grows outraged by trusted mechanic David Puddy's theft of his best sex "move." Frank Costanza, meanwhile, has an unfortunate but memorable medical mishap. A special Emmy to Jason Alexander for George's pronunciation of the word *coherence* during the discussion with his mother about whether or not she's "out there" in the dating world. Patrick Warburton makes a strong impression here as David Puddy, and will go on to become a ninth-season fixture.

102. THE DIPLOMAT
Initial Airdate: May 4, 1995

One of *Seinfeld*'s sharpest looks at the state of race relations, "The Diplomat" finds George going out of his way not to seem like a racist after making an offhand comment about how his boss, Morgan (Tom Wright), resembles a certain sports star. George's search for a black stand-in friend is hysterical in its liberal Caucasian desperation. Debra Jo Rupp is appropriately ass-kissing as Jerry's college-tour agent Katie with whom the comedian shares far too much of a road trip from hell.

103. THE FACE PAINTER
Initial Airdate: May 11, 1995

Move-stealing mechanic David Puddy (Patrick Warburton) of "The Fusilli Jerry" returns. Here he's the title character of "The Face Painter," an episode that goes beyond "The Wave" cheer to bravely explore the contemporary problem of buffoonish behavior at sports events and the resulting humiliation that can follow in its aftermath for those who must sit in nearby seats. George finally says he loves another human, only to find that his words go unanswered.

Puddy is a devoted New Jersey Devils hockey fan. What is the Devils' home venue?

    a. Madison Square Garden
    b. The Meadowlands
    c. The Nassau County Coliseum
    d. The Improv

104. THE UNDERSTUDY

Initial Airdate: May 18, 1995

A funny and inside backstage trip into the theater world written by Carol Leifer and the late Marjorie Gross, "The Understudy" finds Jerry dating Bette Midler's ambitious understudy in *Rochelle Rochelle: The Musical.* Elaine meets up with J. Peterman, her blustering boss-to-be played by John O'Hurley with pleasing portentiousness and self-satisfied machismo, and also quite accidentally ends up reuniting Frank Costanza with an old love.

Which of the following is not a movie in which Bette Midler appears?

    a. *Scenes from a Mall*
    b. *Ruthless People*
    c. *Hawaii*
    d. *Rochelle Rochelle*

THE SEVENTH SEASON

105. THE ENGAGEMENT

Initial Airdate: September 21, 1995

This historic season-opening episode "The Engagement," written by Larry David, represents a dangerous if comfortingly transitory brush with maturity as Jerry and George break character and agree that the time has come to grow up and become men. Foolishly, George, in a shining performance by Alexander, takes this pact to heart and out of the blue gets engaged to Susan. Meanwhile, Elaine less originally finds herself dogged by serious noise problems.

Heidi Swedberg—who played Susan Biddle Ross—also appeared in the cast of which of the following sitcoms?
   a. *Roc*
   b. *Boy Meets World*
   c. *Married . . . With Children*
   d. *Brotherly Love*

106. THE POSTPONEMENT

Initial Airdate: September 28, 1995

Looking for a little of that new-time religion? "The Postponement" boasts one controversial character well worth waiting around for: a rather chatty rabbi who's singularly incapable of keeping a confidence. That's not your standard sitcom cliché, and perhaps as a result this episode elicited plenty of angry letters as well as lots of laughs. Elaine confesses to the rabbi (hilariously played by Larry David and Michael Richards's onetime *Fridays* colleague Bruce Mahler) her mixed feelings about George's impending nuptials. Kramer spills a hot drink and seeks a legal remedy.

107. THE MAESTRO

Initial Airdate: October 5, 1995

Ever vigilant in his seemingly neverending journey to justice, famed fictional attorney Jackie Chiles makes a splash on the *Seinfeld* scene when he

SEINING OFF
JENNY MCCARTHY on *Seinfeld*

MTV's post-grunge dating show **Singled Out** *helped single out this former* **Playboy** *pinup for mainstream success. She's gone on to her own MTV sketch comedy series,* **The Jenny McCarthy Show,** *and more recently* **Jenny,** *an NBC sitcom that made her a network colleague of Jerry and company. Here we find she's more than willing to stick her neck and famous tongue out as a fan of* **Seinfeld** *in general and of laugh-riot grrrl Elaine in particular.*

I'm an *enormous, huge Seinfeld* fan. I'm a total Elainehead. She's so full of trouble, always struggling, and I think that's what people love to see. She's always looking for a guy and the guy always turns out to be some psycho weirdo. And she always runs into psycho people at work too. The character, and the way she plays the character, blow my mind. She seriously goes on one of those lists with Carol Burnett and Lucille Ball.

Andy Ackerman, who directed our pilot and who directs *Seinfeld*, has invited me to come down to introduce me to the cast. And I'm most excited about meeting Julia Louis-Dreyfus—she's just so good. And you can tell why I would like her because she's kinda physical—when she says "Get out" and pushes the guys, that's me. She influenced me in her freedom. I hate to name a favorite episode because they're all so good. I loved "The Muffin Tops" recently. And when she was dating the guy with no hair. And maybe my favorite is "The English Patient." But every episode cracks you up. It's absolutely the model for what a sitcom can be today.

comes in to argue Kramer's case against Java World for injuries sustained back in "The Postponement." And you thought *Cochran & Grace* was a laugh riot. George makes a stir when he stands up for a security guard who he feels should sit down, and we are introduced to Kramer's pretentious classical conductor buddy, who goes by the name "Maestro."

Mark Metcalf—who plays the Maestro—had which of the following roles in a renowned screen comedy smash?

   a. Doug Niedermeyer in *Animal House*
   b. The Robot in *Sleeper*
   c. Arthur in *Arthur*
   d. The gopher in *Caddyshack*

108. THE WINK

Initial Airdate: October 12, 1995

While not a dog of an episode, "The Wink" is only hit-and-miss funny as Elaine dates a canine-loving wake-up-service worker and Jerry fakes a love for mutton so that he can curry favor with Elaine's cuddly carnivore cousin Holly. Grapefruit-induced winking gets George into a little trouble. And in an inventively unsentimental update of a legendary Babe Ruth story, Kramer promises that a Yankee will hit two home runs for a sick kid.

109. THE HOT TUB

Initial Airdate: October 19, 1995

Warning: You'll want to spend no more than thirty minutes in "The Hot Tub," which doesn't exactly overflow with memorable moments. For a situation comedy that is routinely timely, *Seinfeld* sure features a lot of storylines about characters who oversleep—this time it's a late wake-up for Jean-Paul from Haiti, Elaine's speedy houseguest who has come to town in order to compete in the New York City Marathon. Kramer takes a memorable dip in a hot tub.

True or false: The New York City Marathon runs right by Jerry's apartment at 121 West 81st Street.

110. THE SOUP NAZI

Initial Airdate: November 2, 1995

No, it's not springtime for Hitler again—the title character in this culinary comedy classic written by Spike Feresten isn't an anti-Semite, just a temperamental yet top-notch chef who's mastered attitude from soup to nuts. Based partly on an actual New York City food facility, "The Soup Nazi" deals with the vaguely authoritarian behavior exhibited by the owner (Larry Thomas), which is put up with by the huddled hungry masses yearning to eat soup. Kramer allows Elaine's new cabinet to get stolen by some curiously effeminate thugs.

True or false: Al Yegenah, the real person on whom the Soup Nazi is based, is a close friend and personal chef of Jerry Seinfeld.

111. THE SECRET CODE

Initial Airdate: November 9, 1995

Intimacy and banking issues add up to lots of comic interest in "The Secret Code" as George refuses to reveal the deep, dark secret of his bank machine code to Susan. Jason Alexander is certainly the star of the episode as a horrified and excuseless George finds himself stuck not only having dinner with Peterman, but also going to the deathbed of the long-winded one's elderly mother.

John O'Hurley and Jason Alexander have so much chemistry—why not lengthen their meal to a full-length feature: *My Dinner with Peterman?*

In "The Secret Code," Jerry offends an electronics tycoon named Leapin' Larry, played by Lewis Arquette, who also appeared on which beloved family TV series?
  a. *The Waltons*
  b. *Little House on the Prairie*
  c. *Father Knows Best*
  d. *Married with Children*

112. THE POOL GUY
Initial Airdate: November 16, 1995

Alternate title: *When Worlds Collide.* With all the male bonding in *Seinfeld,* Elaine realizes in the David Mandel–written "The Pool Guy" that she has no female friends and then—much to the chagrin of George—decides to strike up a friendship with Susan Biddle Ross. This new development threatens to upset the entire order of things. Jerry gets his own unwanted new pal in the form of the title character. And in a slightly gimmicky best-guffaw-worthy subplot, Kramer gets a wave of phone calls looking for movie information.

Jerry wears a shirt in "The Pool Guy" from the real Jerry's alma mater. What college did Jerry Seinfeld attend?
  a. Smith
  b. Queens College
  c. Massapequa University
  d. Georgetown

113. THE SPONGE
Initial Airdate: December 7, 1995

Who said *Seinfeld* isn't a sexually responsible show? Though, as always, there's nothing safe about the comedy in *Seinfeld,* as "The Sponge" finds Elaine stockpiling her chosen form of birth control when she's outraged to discover the Today sponge is being discontinued. Jerry worries that he may be dating a woman who is too admirable. Kramer causes an uproar by refusing to wear a ribbon at an AIDS walk, where he runs into some familiar trouble from "The Soup Nazi."

114. THE GUM
Initial Airdate: December 14, 1995

In the somewhat flavorless "The Gum," Kramer gets involved in bringing back an old movie theater—hey, somebody's gotta provide a venue for a *Trial & Error* revival—while Jerry must wear glasses because of a fib from Elaine. And, go figure, George gets confused for a man on the verge of a nervous breakdown. Significant historical moment: George dressed as Henry the Eighth.

What wildly gifted writer turns up in a cameo appearance as a newsstand man in "The Gum"?
a. John Updike
b. John Cheever
c. Charles Dickens
d. Larry David

115. THE RYE

Initial Airdate: January 4, 1996

"The Rye" is an especially fresh, chewy and wry gem of a *Seinfeld* episode written by Carol Leifer. In a sort of Kenny G–spot subplot, Elaine's hot new beau is a slick jazz saxophonist who's not willing to perform a certain sort of solo. A marble rye is at the center of trouble between the Costanzas and the Rosses, and Kramer gets into the horse-drawn carriage business for a smelly spell.

116. THE CADDY

Initial Airdate: January 25, 1996

Before the great Tiger Woods explosion, golf had a very different yet still gripping on-screen spokesman in the form of Cosmo Kramer. In the far from subpar "The Caddy," Kramer

begins to rely too much on the advice of his caddy Stan (Armin Shimerman). George is more than happy when he gets confused for being a hard worker by the Yankees—until he's given up for dead.

117. THE SEVEN

Initial Airdate: February 1, 1996

Do the clothes make the woman? Well, apparently in *Seinfeld* they do, at least in "The Seven," when Jerry becomes extremely freaked out by the fact that his otherwise appealing new girlfriend, Christie, seems to wear only one outfit over and over again. Elaine strains her neck and George becomes excessively territorial about a name he has picked out for his own future spawn—Seven. No actor owns possessiveness better than Alexander, which he brilliantly displays in "The Seven."

118. THE CADILLAC

Initial Airdate: February 8, 1996

Like a lot of one-hour episodes, "The Cadillac" runs out of gas a little early. In this comfortable but not especially luxurious one-hour ride, "The Cadillac" finds Jerry deciding to buy his parents a brand-new Cadillac, but Morty gets wrongly accused of embezzlement because of the generous act. The chance to get set up with a popular film actress makes George feel even less certain about the whole engagement-to-Susan thing, while Kramer does battle with the cable company.

While Georgie Boy would be jealous of his real counterpart, Jason Alexander, which movie really did feature both the appealing Marisa Tomei and Alexander?
  a. *Deconstructing Harry*
  b. *Pretty Woman*
  c. *The Paper*
  d. *My Cousin Newman*

Actor Bill Macy plays Herb, one of Morty and Helen's Florida neighbors in "The Cadillac." What highly influential sitcom of the past starred Macy?
  a. *Herman's Head*
  b. *Maude*
  c. *The Munsters*
  d. *Bosom Buddies*

119. THE SHOWER HEAD
Initial Airdate: February 15, 1996

"The Shower Head" does the job despite being slightly drippy. Elaine's physical for a trip with Peterman suggests that she's on drugs when she's really just addicted to poppy-seed muffins. Jerry and Kramer unhappily cope with the lousy new water-saving shower heads

put into their apartment building. The comic high point here is watching the feuding Costanzas and Seinfelds face off and get territorial to fine effect.

120. THE DOLL
Initial Airdate: February 22, 1996

A Freudian field day is had when Susan's doll—which bears an uncanny resemblance to George's mom—understandably causes serious performance problems for Georgie Boy. Because of Sally (Kathy Griffin)—Susan's old pal who works for FedEx—Jerry is missing the saucy prop he has planned on using for a television appearance with Charles Grodin. Kathy Griffin stands out despite her slightly silly role in this minor episode.

Kathy Griffin, who plays the lady from FedEx in "The Doll," currently can be seen in the cast of what NBC series?
  a. *Suddenly Susan*
  b. *Mad About You*
  c. *Caroline in the City*
  d. *Frasier*

Hair Today: The gang endures a really bad hair day in "The Shower Head."

121. THE FRIARS CLUB
Initial Airdate: March 7, 1996

"The Friars Club" may be more lively than most of the Club's actual roasts and with significantly less threat of heartburn. A *Men Behaving Badly* star is a man behaving deafly in "The Friars Club," an episode that also finds Jerry seeking membership in the famous showbizzy club of the title but having a jacket mishap. George and Susan's engagement is on hold here, and Kramer artfully patterns his sleep habits after those of fellow renaissance man Leonardo da Vinci.

Which of the following real-life entertainers does not appear in "The Friars Club"?
   a. The Flying Karamazov Brothers
   b. Pat Cooper
   c. Rob Schneider
   d. Chumbawamba

122. THE WIG MASTER
Initial Airdate: April 4, 1996

Prostitution has rarely provided so much good clean fun as it does in "The Wig Master" when George discovers that the world's oldest profession is practiced in his car in a parking lot, where the rates aren't the only thing that's cheap. This excellent episode written by Spike Feresten ("The Soup Nazi") also finds Elaine with more dating woes involving a Brit. Kramer gets to live out every

Andrew Lloyd Webber lover's dream— the chance to wear that still amazing "Dreamcoat."

Which former seventies icon has played Joseph in Andrew Lloyd Webber's Joseph and the Amazing Technicolor Dreamcoat?
   a. Peter Frampton
   b. Jermaine Jackson
   c. Donny Osmond
   d. Leif Garrett

Patrick Bristow—who plays Ethan, the wig master for a touring production of Joseph and the Amazing Technicolor Dreamcoat, *in "The Wig Master"—has been a featured player on which of the following TV shows?*
   a. *Ellen*
   b. *The Simpsons*
   c. *Walker, Texas Ranger*
   d. *America's Most Wanted*

123. THE CALZONE
Initial Airdate: April 25, 1996

Far from the usual cheesy sitcom stuff, the particularly tasty "The Calzone" confronts funny food issues as George is responsible for taking care of George Steinbrenner's lunchtime cravings (Steinbrenner is once again deliciously voiced by Larry David). This arrangement goes wrong when George gets banned from the pizzeria. Elaine has a boyfriend who has trouble committing even to the idea that they are dating.

George Steinbrenner, whose name will forever be linked to the Yankees—and Seinfeld—*is well-known in what other sporting circles?*
    a. Horse racing
    b. Shot-putting
    c. Synchronized swimming
    d. Manager removal

124. THE BOTTLE DEPOSIT
Initial Airdate: May 2, 1996

You won't necessarily demand a cash refund after sucking down "The Bottle Deposit," but this is a one-hour episode that had about a half hour's worth of great ideas. "The Bottle Deposit" finds Kramer and Newman scheming to cash in and Jerry dealing with a nutsy car repairman who gets *way* too involved with his work. Elaine, who has a way of tangling with the Kennedys, overpays for JFK's golf clubs for Peterman at the Kennedy auction.

Brad Garrett—who plays Tony, the oddly possessive mechanic, in "The Bottle Deposit"—can be seen in the cast of which currently acclaimed sitcom?
    a. *The Nanny*
    b. *Jenny*
    c. *Everybody Loves Raymond*
    d. *Unhappily Ever After*

125. THE WAIT OUT
Initial Airdate: May 9, 1996

Good old-fashioned predatory romance is at the heart of the wonderfully mean-spirited "The Wait Out," an episode written by Peter Mehlman and Matt Selman in which Jerry and Elaine go on the attack in tag-team style so that they can score—individually, that is—with Beth (Debra Messing) and David (Cary Elwes), a newly split up, attractive couple. Fashion maven Kramer makes a too-tight-denim fashion statement.

Debra Messing plays Beth, the female half of the couple Jerry and Elaine attempt to split up in "The Wait Out." Which of the following is a show she starred in?
    a. *Ned & Stacey*
    b. *The Mothers-in-Law*
    c. *Sha Na Na*
    d. *Kato & Kompany*

126. THE INVITATIONS
Initial Airdate: May 16, 1996

"Wedding Bell Blues" could be an alternate title for this invitingly wicked episode—Larry David's last to date—in which George moves precariously close to marital bliss or some less blissful facsimile thereof. Reportedly, scenes shot with the real George Steinbrenner were ultimately cut from "The Invitations." Also cut in a sense here is Susan Biddle Ross, who takes a licking and drops dead due to George's thrifty—read *cheap*—taste in wedding invitation envelopes. Jerry also meets Jeannie, the woman of his dreams—basically a prettier version of him.

Who plays Jerry's amazingly simpatico *girlfriend, Jeannie Steinman, in "The Invitations"?*
a. Janeane Garofalo
b. Ellen DeGeneres
c. Carol Channing
d. Shoshanna Lonstein

Couplehood: George and Susan
try to lick their problems.

THE EIGHTH SEASON

127. THE FOUNDATION

Initial Airdate: September 19, 1996

One need not be in a charitable mood to embrace "The Foundation," this season opener by Alec Berg and Jeff Schaeffer, as a comic gem. This seems an especially impressive episode, since it's the first post–Larry David show. We find George not grappling with the loss of Susan, but instead coping with the hassle of having to be on the foundation that bears her name. Elaine finds herself with a job upgrade, and Kramer enters the world of martial arts.

Bruce Davison plays Mr. Wyck, who runs the foundation to honor Susan Biddle Ross. Which of the following is not *a film in which Davison had a major role?*
   a. *Willard*
   b. *The Crucible*
   c. *Longtime Companion*
   d. *Eight Heads in a Duffel Bag*

128. THE SOUL MATE

Initial Airdate: September 26, 1996

Even Jerry Lewis would have to laugh at this guilt-ridden episode in which Jason Alexander plays George at his paranoid best when he goes to unorthodox, nearly Nixonian lengths to find out if the Susan Biddle Ross Foundation members think that he intentionally killed Susan. Elaine gets involved with a fellow named Kevin who will feature in the alternative realities of the upcoming even more humorous "The Bizarro Jerry." Kramer and Jerry like the same girl.

129. THE BIZARRO JERRY

Initial Airdate: October 3, 1996

"The Bizarro Jerry" is like a trip to *The Twilight Zone* on laughing gas. In this imaginative and hilarious episode written by David Mandel, Elaine starts hanging out with a gang that appears to be a better-adjusted mutation of Jerry, George and Kramer—sort of like how those three would have ended up in the hands of your average sitcom hacks if

"The Pilot" had been picked up. Even better is Kramer's brief field trip into the corporate world, especially the fantastic bit of physical comedy when we see Cosmo enjoying a big after-work laugh with all his new work pals—arguably this author's single favorite Kramer moment.

130. THE LITTLE KICKS
Initial Airdate: October 10, 1996

Certain *Seinfeld* moments are forever emblazoned in our consciousness. "Sweet fancy Moses," we, as well as George, can say when a dangerous and frankly frightening case of dance fever overcomes the usually cool Elaine in "The Little Kicks." Like her shocked colleagues, we the viewers lose a little bit of respect for Elaine when we see that on the dance floor she's clearly a mover and a shaker with absolutely all the wrong moves. Also memorable and insightful is George's attempt—successful for a while—to be a seductive bad boy so that he can win over Anna, one of Elaine's fetching colleagues at J. Peterman.

131. THE PACKAGE
Initial Airdate: October 17, 1996

Elaine somehow manages to alienate nearly as many doctors as managed health care has in "The Package," an

episode I would have to diagnose as slightly anemic. The high point here—such as it is—is George's amusing attempt to get things rolling romantically with a very attractive photo store worker, Sheila (Heather Campbell), but finally he ends up turning on the wrong store employee.

132. THE FATIGUES
Initial Airdate: October 31, 1996

You don't have to be Jewish to enjoy "The Fatigues," but it couldn't hurt. Always one who enjoys a nosh and a little friendly kibitzing, Kramer gets into the business of hosting a Jewish singles get-together in "The Fatigues," leading indirectly to a haunting wartime food flashback for cooking vet Mr. Costanza, while Elaine deals with another crazed vet at work. A horrified Jerry discovers his new girlfriend's much-discussed mentor is currently dating the always fatiguing Bania.

133. THE CHECKS
Initial Airdate: November 7, 1996

"The Checks" is a modestly bouncing and hospitable affair that's sort of like *Seinfeld at Budokan*—a strong Far Eastern flavor comes across here as Jerry gets a big payday from an appearance abroad, and Kramer somehow ends up running a rooming house for Japanese tourists in the relatively cramped quarters of his apartment. Meanwhile, witchy woman Elaine dates Brett, an annoying character who is super-possessive about the Eagles' well-worn standard "Desperado."

134. THE CHICKEN ROASTER
Initial Airdate: November 14, 1996

There's nothing poultry about the comic results of "The Chicken Roaster," which comes from the pens of Alec Berg and Jeff Schaffer. The presence of a new Kenny Rogers Roasters chicken spot across the street becomes a nuisance, then a full-blown addiction issue for Kramer in this moderately flavorful TV dinner. Having shopped too much on the corporate dime, Elaine is sent to Burma.

135. THE ABSTINENCE
Initial Airdate: November 21, 1996

Lack of sex pays impressive intellectual dividends in "The Abstinence," a quick-witted episode even by *Seinfeld*'s lofty standards as George happens upon a fascinating cerebral phenomenon: It turns out that he gets smarter and smarter as long as he doesn't score in bed. Elaine—who certainly seems to have a lot of trouble with the medical community—dates a man who is ever so close to being a real doctor. Returning to his junior high, Jerry has career day booking problems, while Kramer puffs on a smoky subplot, in this Steven Koren–written episode.

Bob Odenkirk—who plays Elaine's near-doctor beau in "The Abstinence"—is one of the great comic talents in which of the following acclaimed comedy groups?
  a. The State
  b. Kids in the Hall
  c. Mr. Show
  d. The Firesign Theater

136. THE ANDREA DORIA
Initial Airdate: December 19, 1996

Far from a titanic shipwreck of an episode, "The Andrea Doria" offers some likably odd comic historical revisionism as George attempts to show he's had a tougher life than an aged survivor of the sinking of the famed *Andrea Doria* so he can impress a tenant board and score a bigger pad. Never one to doggedly follow doctors' orders, Kramer attempts to heal himself with canine medicine.

Unmanageable Health Care:
Elaine has major medical issues
in "The Package."

137. THE LITTLE JERRY
Initial Airdate: January 9, 1997

Chained Heat meets Upper West Side neurosis in "The Little Jerry," a strong episode written by Jennifer Crittenden which is most arresting during George's behind-prison-walls love affair with Celia. All is well until Celia breaks free. Animal rights advocates be damned, Jerry's new rooster—the episode's title character—has a close brush with the poorly documented underworld of deli-sponsored cockfighting.

138. THE MONEY
Initial Airdate: January 16, 1997

Though there is no Alan Greenspan guest spot, financial panic nonetheless runs rampant on the Black Thursday that is "The Money." The perennially self-interested George ponders the Costanzas' spending habits and their eventual impact on his own bottom line, while Jerry's folks misconstrue his fiscal health and worry about their beloved son's savings. Elaine, meanwhile, experiences some extremely depressing downward mobility at her workplace, in an episode that's satisfying but not richly so.

139. THE COMEBACK
Initial Airdate: January 30, 1997

Hilarious only in spurts, "The Comeback," written by Gregg Kavet and Andy Robin, finds George in his natural mental habitat, completely over-thinking things, as he makes a bit of a "jerk store" of himself. Less amusing is Jerry's encounter with a lousy yet curiously arrogant tennis player, and Elaine blindly flirts on the phone with a film buff.

140. THE VAN BUREN BOYS
Initial Airdate: February 6, 1997

As gangs go, the title group in "The Van Buren Boys" come off as being relatively benign but also, sadly, pretty unfunny. There are some strong elements to this episode, especially George's campaign for the like-minded young Steven to win the foundation scholarship despite his minimal qualifications. Jerry dates another seemingly perfect but ultimately flawed woman. And in an apparent reference to a recent Jay Leno anecdote-purchasing incident, Peterman purchases some of Kramer's colorful anecdotes for his autobiography.

Christine Taylor, who plays Jerry's love interest, Ellen, in "The Van Buren Boys," played which of the following roles in The Brady Bunch Movie?
   a. Alice the maid
   b. Sam the butcher
   c. Tiger the dog
   d. Marcia Brady

141. THE SUSIE

Initial Airdate: February 13, 1997

"The Susie" finds things getting even stranger and less professional than usual at the J. Peterman office as Elaine gets confused with a fictional colleague named Susie, who still ends up having a rather well-attended funeral by the end of this David Mandel–scripted episode. George saves the entire less-than-stellar thirty minutes with an extraordinary phone–answering machine message that features a musical nod to the theme from *The Greatest American Hero.*

Before George made the song his own, which of the following performers sang the smash version of "Believe It or Not," the opening theme song from The Greatest American Hero?
   a. Leonard Cohen
   b. Nick Cave
   c. Morrissey
   d. Joey Scarbury

142. THE POTHOLE

Initial Airdate: February 20, 1997

Bumpy and not too deep, "The Pothole" features *Melrose Place* diva Kristin Davis as the lovely young lady whom Jerry just can't bring himself to kiss because of her fallen (in the toilet) toothbrush. Elaine—apparently not one for cooking at home much—has yet more issues with Chinese food–delivery as she goes way out of her way for a favorite fish dish on which she's become hooked. Also, Kramer becomes something of a highwayman.

What was the name of the now–deceased character Kristin Davis played on that notably nonhygienic show Melrose Place?
   a. Brooke
   b. Billy
   c. Allison
   d. The courtyard pool

143. THE ENGLISH PATIENT

Initial Airdate: March 13, 1997

Never a series to bow to general consensus, *Seinfeld* deserves a special Oscar for Elaine's brave performance here in this Steven Koren–penned episode as the lone holdout from loving *The English Patient.* In Florida, Jerry gets stuck dealing with Lloyd Bridges, who plays crepe king Izzy Mandelbaum. And there's another cigar-related subplot. In addition to all its healthier accomplishments, has *Seinfeld* helped make cigars hip again?

144. THE NAP
Initial Airdate: April 10, 1997

In "The Nap," *Seinfeld* appears to be under construction during an unusually sleepy and slow-building episode. Jerry has some remodeling done in his kitchen, which predictably does not go well. Comfort freak George, tired from staying up watching *The Omen*, has more luck with the custom-built sleep chamber he has a carpenter create for him, until he gets trapped there in a memorable, miserable Yankee moment.

In "The Nap," the George Steinbrenner character sings a song from which eighties pop star?
   a. Madonna
   b. Joan Jett
   c. Pat Benatar
   d. Juice Newton

145. THE YADA YADA
Initial Airdate: April 24, 1997

Just a brief "yada yada" cannot suffice to explain this excellent episode of few words but lots of laughs, which was written by Peter Mehlman and Jill Franklyn.

George's new love interest here, Marcy (Suzanne Cryer), is a woman of poor moral character who still makes a tremendous contribution to the *Seinfeld* vocabulary with the title phrase. The other notable storyline here involves the biting issue of "anti-dentite" behavior, as Jerry becomes suspicious of dentist Tim Whatley's religious conversion.

146. THE MILLENNIUM
Initial Airdate: May 1, 1997

Throughout much of *Seinfeld* history, failing was not a particularly difficult thing for Georgie Boy to do—you might say he was a natural at it. In "The Millennium," however, George must get himself fired by the Yankees so that he can move on and take a great job with the New York Mets. Amazingly, he has trouble screwing up. Elaine has gigantic trouble with a Putumayo saleslady (Victoria Mahoney) and Kramer plans a big fin de siècle shindig, only to discover that he'll be competing with Newman. Like the last thousand years of history, "The Millennium" is a hit-or-miss affair.

147. THE MUFFIN TOPS
Initial Airdate: May 8, 1997

An alternative title for "The Muffin Tops" could be "The Out-of-Towner," since the comedic high point here is

George faking being a "hen supervisor" and non–New Yorker so that he can continue seeing Mary Anne, a highly accommodating and attractive employee of the city's Visitors' Bureau. The muffin-top subplot is not tasty enough by half and grows stale eventually, despite the return of Mr. Lippman. Anyone who has had the pleasure of taking Kenny Kramer's Reality Tour will love the none too subtle in-joke of Cosmo Kramer's awfully similar "The Real Peterman Reality Tour."

What will you not *see on Kenny Kramer's Reality Tour?*
   a. Tom's Diner (the real Monk's Diner)
   b. Soup Kitchen International (the real Soup Nazi)
   c. The Costanza home in Queens
   d. The real Junior Mint hospital

148. THE SUMMER OF GEORGE
Initial Airdate: May 15, 1997

This hot season closer offers another inspired night at the theater. In "The Summer of George," Kramer somehow wrongly grabs a Tony Award and ends up having to fire difficult diva Raquel Welch from a production of *Scarsdale Surprise*. There's also another crazed stalker on *Seinfeld,* only this time around it's a woman—Elaine's colleague Sam (played with deranged gusto by *Saturday Night Live*'s Molly Shannon). Oh, the joy of watching catfights. As for the show's title, an especially lazy George takes a summer internship helping Jerry with his newly trying personal life.

Cigar aficionado Kramer lights up
another episode.

THE NINTH SEASON

149. THE BUTTER SHAVE
Initial Airdate: September 25, 1997

Aired the same night as NBC's over-hyped live episode of *ER*, this fine season-opener episode proved far livelier. "The Butter Shave" had something to offend everyone, not only the handicapped—nice Stephen Hawkings joke—but also all cannibals due to the new link here with hungry man Newman. Kramer gets buttered and burnt, and frequent flyer Elaine has a bad time in Europe with former face painter David Puddy. As for the former pride of the Yankees, George Costanza briefly goes to work for Play Now playground equipment.

Who plays George's boss at the Play Now playground equipment company in "The Butter Shave"?
  a. Judd Hirsch of *Taxi*
  b. Gordon Jump of *WKRP in Cincinnati*
  c. Donny Most of *Happy Days*
  d. George Steinbrenner of the New York Yankees

150. THE VOICE
Initial Airdate: October 2, 1997

The increasingly popular David Puddy returns in this on-again, off-again episode, which elaborates on Puddy and Elaine's equally uneven relationship. George and Jerry share a running gag about his girlfriend's talking stomach, and Jerry picks the voice over the girl, which is good because the voice grows as annoying to the viewer as it does to George and Kramer. Kramer hilariously attempts to get Kramerica Industries up and going again, this time with the dedicated assistance of Darin (Jarrad Paul), an intern from NYU.

151. THE SERENITY NOW
Initial Airdate: October 9, 1997

"The Serenity Now" is a historic, unusually emotional episode marked by mantra madness and the aftermath of Jerry's breakup with Patty (Lori Loughlin), which temporarily leaves our title character a veritable wuss, proclaiming his love for George and proposing to Elaine. For those of us who have been

SEINING OFF
RICK RUBIN on *Seinfeld*

A groundbreaking rap and rock producer and record executive who has worked with the Beastie Boys, LL Cool J, Tom Petty and the Red Hot Chili Peppers, among many others, Rubin is also a major Seinfeld *booster. Indeed, this chairman of the boards and noted tastemaker has been known to stop recording sessions so as not to miss the latest rocking adventures of one of his very favorite groups—Jerry, George, Elaine and Kramer.*

I think *Seinfeld* is probably the best show ever in the history of television. There's *Lucy*, which I love, and *Taxi*, which is clearly great, but I think because of the number of important characters and the intertwining storylines, you can't really compare *Seinfeld* with something like *I Love Lucy*. A great *Seinfeld* is really like four *I Love Lucy*s. If anything the show is rooted in *The Abbott and Costello Show*—another one of my favorites. *Seinfeld*'s got some of the same kind of nonlinear, surrealistic, mean-spirited humor.

During the recording of the last Red Hot Chili Peppers album and on Tom Petty's *Wild-flowers* album, we would definitely stop everything and watch *Seinfeld*. I still actively watch the show, and I'm not a television watcher. For me *Seinfeld* is caricature—it's reality taken to a further extreme, whereas most shows are not based on reality at all. I think my favorite episode of the show is "The Marine Biologist." I've actually seen the masturbation episode dubbed in Italian, and it was *really* interesting seeing it in another language. It feels like a foreign film. It actually felt very European.

I think the difference between *Seinfeld* and television in general as a medium is that television tends to be lowest-common-denominator entertainment and doesn't respect the audience at all. *Seinfeld* completely respects its audience. It's funny that George, in the "jerk store" episode, says, "I'm not dumbing down my material for the masses." And that's what *Seinfeld* doesn't do.

watching him all along, it's a little sweet but disturbing to watch Jerry emote. Elaine copes with her tribal appeal when Mr. Lippman's son gets bar mitzvahed—dig the chatty rabbi redux. The title phrase comes from a relaxation tech-

nique employed by Frank Costanza and Kramer with predictably little success.

Lori Loughlin, who spent many years as former soap star John Stamos's girlfriend and wife on Full House, *was herself in a*

soap opera. Which soap opera helped make
Loughlin a television star?

a. *General Hospital*
b. *The Edge of Night*
c. *The Bold and the Beautiful*
d. *Heaving Bosoms High*

152. THE BLOOD
Initial Airdate: October 16, 1997

Sadly, a weighty episode in one sense and one sense only—"The Blood" finds Jerry's folks in town, and they tell him he's gained a few pounds, so they bring in Izzy Mandelbaum (Lloyd Bridges), a returning character from "The English Patient," for some personal training. Kramer has hematologically humorous banking problems with the blood bank.

153. THE JUNK MAIL
Initial Airdate: October 30, 1997

Kramer takes on Pottery Barn for sending him so many catalogs in this not entirely junky Spike Feresten–scripted episode. Driven to the edge—not much of a trip—he starts an antimail campaign that eventually lands him in trouble with the Postmaster General. George feels his folks are avoiding him—and as it turns out, he's right. Jerry's old pal Frankie (Dana Gould) gives him a van that the lusty Costanzas eventually get

a-rockin' (they still have it after all these years).

Who plays the mildly menacing Postmaster General in "The Junk Mail"?

a. Anthony Quinn
b. Fred Thompson
c. Wilford Brimley
d. Lorna Luft

154. THE MERV GRIFFIN SHOW
Initial Airdate: November 6, 1997

Kramer catches the talk show bug to hysterical effect in "The Merv Griffin Show" in which he—ever the obsessive pop culture scavenger—discovers Merv's hallowed old set, puts it up in his apartment and proceeds to restart the festivities for a select audience. Hey, his talk show did better than Chevy Chase's brief attempt. Jerry, meanwhile, becomes almost erotically fixated on the toy collection of gal pal Celia (Julia Pennington).

What animal authority makes a cameo appearance as a guest on Kramer's chat show in "The Merv Griffin Show"?

a. Jim Fowler
b. Marlin Perkins
c. Dian Fossey
d. Dr. Doolittle

155. THE SLICER
Initial Airdate: November 13, 1997

A lean little comedy, "The Slicer"—written by Steven Koren—finds Kramer trading in his sausage press for a professional meat slicer. George is driven to desperate measures—as usual—to save his job. Jerry prematurely mocks a dedicated dermatologist (Marcia Cross of *Melrose Place* fame). For *Seinfeld* swingers everywhere, "The Slicer" is most notable for Elaine's nightmare sequence, which finds her in the sack with Jerry, George and Kramer.

156. THE BETRAYAL
Initial Airdate: November 20, 1997

This too heavily hyped "backward" episode, more ambitious than amusing, was no masterpiece any way that you run it. Still, once you get past the Pinteresque gimmick, "The Betrayal" tells the story of a moderately funny passage to India for the wedding of Sue Ellen, where sexual secrets come back to haunt Elaine and Jerry. Meanwhile, back in the U.S.A., FDR—Franklin Delano Romanowski, naturally—wants Kramer to drop dead for his birthday wish. Watching "The Betrayal" is like watching a good episode of *Seinfeld* in Hebrew.

157. THE APOLOGY
Initial Airdate: December 11, 1997

Yeah sure, you've heard of a naked lunch, but in the atypically fleshy and slightly flabby "The Apology"—written by Jennifer Crittenden—we see Jerry's most recent girlfriend, Melissa (Kathleen McClellan), enjoy a naked breakfast. The episode shows how jaded Jerry has become—now he gets turned *off* by a pretty naked woman. James Spader makes a strong appearance as Henke, an old acquaintance who's on Step 9 of a 12-step recovery program and making all sorts of apologies—to everyone but George. Kramer tries to cut down on his shower time. Ladies' choice: a rare opportunity to see Jerry topless and surprisingly hairy.

Which of the following is not *a film in which "The Apology" guest star James Spader appears?*
 a. *White Castle*
 b. *Bad Influence*
 c. *Baby Boom*
 d. *Sex, Lies & Estelle Costanza*

158. THE STRIKE
Initial Airdate: December 18, 1997

Happy Festivas, and to all a pretty heart-warming holiday episode written by Dan O'Keefe, Alec Berg and Jeff Schaffer. Gainfully employed *Seinfeld* fans were thrilled—and shocked—to discover that Kramer has held a job when he is *finally* able to return to his work as a bagel technician when a twelve-year-old strike against H&H Bagels is at long last settled. Less charmingly Jerry dates Gwen (Karen Fineman), a woman who is alternately attractive and repellent to him. On the other hand, it's a wonderful life when we learn all about Frank Costanza's homemade holiday and its charming traditions.

159. THE DEALERSHIP
Initial Airdate: January 8, 1998

This first *Seinfeld* episode to air since the general public learned that the show would end at the conclusion of the ninth season, "The Dealership" was no total lemon, but it still remains something of a hard sell on the show floor. The two high points of this Steven Koren–penned show are Jerry switching roles with car salesman Puddy (who's a grease monkey no longer and becoming a real fixture of the season) and Kramer's insane, gas-guzzling test drive of a Saab.

However, George's silly candy war here turns out to be unusually stale stuff.

160. THE REVERSE PEEPHOLE
Initial Airdate: January 15, 1998

Seinfeld has always excelled at looking at things from the other perspective: Here, the ever neighborly tenants Kramer and Newman reverse their peepholes so that people can look *into* their apartments, in this slight but not unlovable episode written by Spike Feresten. The increasingly omnipresent Puddy—who has also started popping up as the voice of the Caped Crusader on Jerry Seinfeld's Superman American Express commercial around this same time—annoys Elaine with his less than macho fur winter coat. The gang gets put to work at the party of Jo Mayo (Pat Finn).

During the first airing of "The Reverse Peephole," Jason Alexander wore a goofy coat in a commercial for which of the following companies?
   a. Hair Club for Men
   b. Intel
   c. Members Only
   d. Kramerica Industries

161. THE CARTOON
Initial Airdate: January 29, 1998

"The Cartoon"—a colorful episode written by Bruce Eric Kaplan—finds the hilariously animated Kathy Griffin returning to *Seinfeld* (she screwed up things for Jerry in "The Doll") as Sally Weaver, Susan's old roommate, a show-biz wanna-be, whom Jerry finds talentless. Elaine grows obsessed with figuring out an elusive *New Yorker* cartoon. George dates Janet, who some folks feel resembles Jerry, and this becomes troubling for George, *not that there's anything wrong with that.*

Which daughter of a famous rock star plays Jerry's supposed doppelgänger, Janet, in "The Cartoon"?
- a. Moon Zappa
- b. Jade Jagger
- c. Liv Tyler
- d. Tracy Nelson

162. THE STRONG BOX
Initial Airdate: February 5, 1998

Talk about timely . . . In this impressively strong episode that first ran just after the execution of ax murderer Karla Faye Tucker, Elaine considers her own last meal possibilities. And with good reason, since she begins to date the man who is her single poorest love interest ever. Neighbor trouble revisits Jerry when he pisses off Phil in 5-E. George encounters a woman with whom he cannot successfully break up.

163. THE WIZARD
Initial Airdate: February 26, 1998

Remember once upon an episode when Kramer went west to find fame and fortune in California? Now, in "The Wizard," *Seinfeld*'s most inspired hair act heads south to the Sunshine State and ends up hanging in the same hood as Jerry's mom and pop. Elaine tries to figure out the racial background of her latest love interest (Samuel Bliss Cooper) when she should really be exploring a more timeless conundrum—how George could possibly *not* be Jewish.

Chained Heat: Kramer behind bars—where arguably he belongs—in "The Trip."

FUTURE SHOCK
The End of *Seinfeld* and the World as We Know It

"Some say the world will end in fire," wrote Robert Frost in his 1923 poem *Fire and Ice;* "Some say in ice." But screw the world, babe; the real pressing question is how the hell will *Seinfeld* end?

As this tribute goes to print, that momentous decision as to the final fate of George, Jerry, Elaine and Kramer was still yet to be made. This much was known: *Seinfeld* cocreator Larry David, who left the show after the 1995–1996 season, would return to write the final send-off. And Jerry Seinfeld has told *Time*'s Bruce Handy not to expect any nuptials for Jerry and Elaine and that the final half hour in sitcom heaven would be accompanied by a mock documentary about the making of the episode. Seinfeld seemed to want to deflate expectations for a final big bang. "It's not a big thing," he said of the finale.

Over the years, the topic of how to end our greatest sitcom has been raised, and the stars have weighed in with their own ideas of how *Seinfeld* will go quietly—or not so quietly—into the night.

"My theory is that Jerry and Elaine will get married one day, but she'll be forty-eight and he'll be fiftysomething," Julia Louis-Dreyfus told *Rolling Stone* in 1993. "Then they'll get divorced six months later." By the same token, in "The Wife," Elaine casually agrees to marry Kramer in fifty years if nothing better pans out for her. Don't hold your breath waiting for that unholy union either.

Though hope springs eternal for the possibility of an *All in the Costanza Family*–style show, there have been multiple denials of such a possible *Seinfeld* spin-off. "I would never do a George spin-off," Alexander told *Today*'s Matt Lauer. "I think when *Seinfeld* is done, George should go to bed."

Then again, since he does have a first name, Jerry Seinfeld could return for a sitcom called *Jerry*, like in "The Pilot." The *Time* interview suggested he'd like to make a film and would even consider returning to television in some form, but not in another sitcom. Though he could well afford to never deliver a punch line again, Seinfeld has also suggested his will *not* be an early retirement. As he told Tom Shales of the *Washington Post* in 1992, "My goal is to be like George Burns, with a little more spinal flexibility."

Finally—true to the dark *Seinfeld* spirit—there have been past intimations of death regarding the logical end of *Seinfeld*. Asked about how the series might wrap things up by *Playboy*'s Bob Daily in 1997, Jason Alexander suggested one possibility had been discussed in which Jerry and Elaine fall madly in love, Kramer finds God and George wins the lottery. And right after Jerry and Elaine wed, they all die.

Louis-Dreyfus addressed the same hellish issue to *US* magazine's Josh Rottenberg, and let us give *Seinfeld*'s leading lady the final word—for now. "There will definitely not be a big group hug, and nobody will be happily ever anything. We joke about what the end should be. Basically, a huge, fiery death." Asked if that meant no ten-year reunion show, Louis-Dreyfus joked, "Yeah, unless it's up in the clouds. (*Pause.*) Actually, I'm not sure it would be up there."

ANSWERS

Answers to "Get Out!"

1. False

2. True

3. True

4. True

5. False

6. False, but may I humbly suggest that he thoroughly deserved one.

7. True

8. False. In fact, Seinfeld told *Playboy*'s David Rensin, "My empire has crumbled."

9. True, or at least that's what Kathie Lee Gifford told Seinfeld during an appearance he made on the *Regis and Kathie Lee* show.

10. False

11. True

12. True

13. True

14. False, though I for one would have paid to see it.

15. False

16. False

17. False

18. True

19. False

20. True

21. False. It was Michael Richards and Larry David's *Fridays* colleague Bruce Mahler.

22. False

23. True

24. False

25. True

26. False

27. True

28. False—in what was for many an upset, Ms. Benes was out of the contest before Jerry and George, and not all that long after Kramer.

29. True

30. True

31. False

32. False. The show has earned the peak position dozens of times.

33. True, at least according to the rigid standards of the fact checkers at that esteemed publication.

34. True

35. True

36. True

37. False

38. True	45. True	52. True
39. True	46. False	53. True
40. False	47. True	54. True
41. True	48. True	55. True
42. False	49. True	56. False
43. True	50. True	
44. False	51. False	

Answers to Episode Questions

To put it mildly, *Seinfeld* has never been hung up with matters of achievement. Still, if you want to keep score, please do so.

2. a	25. c	45. b, d
4. a	26. a	46. c
7. a	27. c	47. d
8. b	28. c	48. b, c
11. c	29. a	49. d
13. c	30. c	52. d
14. a	32. b	53. d
15. c	33. a	55. c
16. a	34. b, b	56. a
18. d	36. b, c	57. c
19. d	38. a	58. c
20. d	39. d	59. b
22. d	40. b, false	60. c
23. c	41. c	61. b
24. c	43. d	62. b

63. b, c	96. b	123. a
65. a	97. c	124. c
67. c	98. b	125. a
68. d	99. true	126. a
70. d	103. b	127. d
71. c	104. d	135. c
73. d, true	105. a	140. d
75. a	107. a	141. d
78. c	109. false	142. a
80. c	110. false	144. c
82. b	111. a	147. c
83. c	112. b	149. b
85. b	114. d	151. b
87. b	118. c, b	153. c
90. c, c	120. a	154. a
91. a	121. d	157. d
95. c	122. c, a	160. b

Answers to "Matchmakers, Matchmakers"

1. h	5. i	9. f
2. b	6. c	10. g
3. a	7. j	
4. d	8. e	

Answers to "Multiple Mishagas"

1. c	10. b	19. a
2. b	11. c	20. d
3. a	12. a	21. b
4. d	13. b	22. d
5. a	14. b	23. c
6. c	15. a	24. b
7. d	16. c	25. a
8. b	17. c	26. d
9. c	18. d	